Read 36-46

THE STOCK MARKET AND ECONOMIC EFFICIENCY

William J. Baumol

THE MILLAR LECTURES · NUMBER SIX · 1965

FORDHAM UNIVERSITY PRESS · NEW YORK

SECOND PRINTING, JANUARY 1969

© FORDHAM UNIVERSITY PRESS . 1965 . NEW YORK

LIBRARY OF CONGRESS CATALOG CARD NUMBER: 65-24469

*To Jacob Viner in gratitude for warm friendship,
impeccable advice and fine cigars.*

Foreword

THE MARKETS FOR STOCKS AND BONDS perform many essential and useful functions in the United States economy. One of the most important is the influence which this market, along with other financial and non-financial institutions, exerts in allocating the nation's capital resources among numerous competing uses for these resources.

The efficiency with which this allocative function is performed determines in large part the overall growth and efficiency of the economy itself. Thus, the government has from time to time passed legislation aimed at improving the performance and efficiency of the stock market.

However, there is still much to be learned about the functioning of the stock market, and in particular about the nature of the price-making process. It is generally recognized that an efficient stock-market should value a company's stock in some way on the basis of the capitalized value of the company's earnings potential. Historical studies on the degree of correlation between market value and earnings should thus provide some indication of stock market performance and efficiency.

It is also revealed in numerous writings that the more closely the stock market corresponds to the classical ideal of perfect competition, the more efficient the market becomes as a resource allocator. Thus, many studies have as their aim the evaluation of the nature of competition existing in the securities markets, and especially in the determination of the nature and extent to which the forces of supply and demand determine price. In this regard, also, the question of whether or not a perfect market is more efficient than some other type of market is sometimes considered.

An additional factor entering into the determination of stock market performance and efficiency is that American enterprise today obtains only a small proportion of its capital needs through new stock issues. Thus, if the stock market is to serve as an efficient allocator of capital in the economy at large, it must somehow exert an influence in the capital markets over which it has no apparent direct control but which nevertheless comprise the bulk of the capital resource available for investment purposes.

The results of statistical analysis of stock market prices reveal that changes in stock prices in the short run are random. These findings not only suggest that short-run prediction is at best a random process, but that largely random factors, and not company earnings, account for price changes. Regarding trends in stock prices, that is, price changes extending over a period of ten years or more, research findings tend to support the view that prices follow roughly the earnings of companies. However, the reasons for this correlation between value and earnings are conflicting. It is clear that further research on this and other aspects of stock market pricing must be done in order to evaluate effectively the efficiency and performance of the stock market.

Professor William J. Baumol, in this volume of the Moorhouse I. X. Millar Lecture Series, makes a number of important contributions toward a better understanding of the performance of the stock market. First, the book represents a synthesis of past research and of current thinking on the subject. Second, drawing upon his own research experience Professor Baumol analyzes in considerable detail both the short-run and long-run price equilibrating processes, and points out important departures from the competitive ideal and the implications of these departures to stock market efficiency. The role of the stock market specialist in the pricing process is particularly well developed. Finally, Professor Baumol offers his own hypothesis on the pricing of securities, and he sheds new light on the overall efficiency of the stock market as a mechanism for allocating the nation's capital resources.

In developing his theme, Professor Baumol has performed a very useful function to the profession. The student and a scholar of economics, and of other disciplines as well, will find here a valuable and penetrating analysis of the stock market pricing process. Indeed, this volume should serve as an indispensable starting point for further work on this subject.

JOSEPH ZAREMBA
Associate Professor of Economics

Department of Economics
Fordham University
July, 1965

Prefatory Note

THE MATERIAL CONSTITUTING THIS VOLUME was delivered at Fordham University as the Millar Lectures for 1964–65. A casual perusal of the book should reveal that they could not have been delivered just as written because of their great variation in length. As a matter of fact, though the manuscript was largely completed before its oral presentation I cannot vouch for the degree of correspondence between the two versions since, in accord with my custom, the talks were delivered extemporaneously.

It must be confessed at the outset that I am primarily an economic theorist and as such have never attained the status of specialist in the institutional arrangements of the stock exchange and the set of lectures therefore adds up largely to a compendium of questions on the workings of the market, questions that would naturally grow out of the theorist's interests and preconceptions.

In writing these essays I was very fortunate to have the knowledge-able assistance of my friend and colleague, Burton Malkiel. Under the circumstances it might almost be appropriate to reverse the usual preface disclaimer by asserting that he must bear blame for any errors of substance which still remain! Thus, his help and the friendly and painstaking prodding provided by Jacob Viner are responsible for any resemblance to the facts.

There are others to whom my debt is also substantial, particularly to Messrs. Nevins Baxter, W. T. Carleton, Thomas Courchene, Michael Godfrey, Stephen Goldfeld, E. M. Lerner, Fritz Machlup, James Meigs, W. E. Miller and R. E. Quandt for their ideas and comments. The National Science Foundation's grant to our project, the Dynamics of the Firm, once more served as an effective means to stimulate and facilitate my work. And, finally, I must thank the Fordham University Department of Economics, and especially Father Hogan, for their kindness, their hospitality, and above all for providing me with the occasion and the stimulus for writing these lectures.[1]

[1] I must also thank the following for permission to quote from their publications: Basil Blackwell & Mott, Limited (I. M. D. Little, "Higgledy Piggledy Growth," the *Bulletin of the Oxford Institute of Statistics*); The Chicago University Press ("Dividend Policy and Market Imperfection," *The Journal of Business*); Division of Research of the Harvard Business School (Gordon Donaldson, *Corporate Debt Capacity*); Harcourt, Brace and World, Inc. (J. M. Keynes, *The General Theory of Employment, Interest and Money*); Harvard University Press (Thomas C. Schelling, *The Strategy of Conflict*); William Hodge and Company (Fritz Machlup, *The Stock Market, Credit and Capital Formation*); Machinery and Allied Products Institute (*Capital Goods Review*); and the Michigan State University Business Studies, Michigan State University (Andrew F. Brimmer, *Life Insurance Companies in the Capital Market*).

Table of Contents

Chapter One

The Platonic Shadow

Ideal Markets and their Imperfect Real

Counterparts

IT SHOULD BE MADE CLEAR at the outset that this book undertakes no systematic analysis of the stock markets' operations and their ramifications. Rather, it deals with several special subjects whose connection is not entirely obvious, and yet which together constitute an overview of some of the markets' most important theoretical properties. It would therefore be undesirable to proceed without providing a guide to the remainder of my materials. As a consequence, this chapter is perhaps condemned to be the least interesting portion of the book, since it is devoted to an outline of my purposes and of the interconnections among the various topics that will be discussed.

Scope of the Discussion

The allocation of its capital resources is among the most important decisions which must be made by any economy. In the long run an appropriate allocation of real capital is absolutely indispensable to the implementation of consumer sovereignty (or of the more appropriate concept—public sovereignty—which takes into account *all* of the relevant desires of the individuals who constitute the economy). For unless the flow of capital goods is responsive to the goals of the members of the public, the community will only be able to exercise a very short-run and temporary control over the composition of output and of its activities. After all, capital is the economy's link with the future and unless our desires can influence the apportionment of capital inputs, our wishes can at most effectively control only today's events.

In addition, the allocation of capital resources plays a critical role in the determination of the rate of growth of the nation's output. If capital resources are not provided to those industries the demand for whose products is growing or is at least expandable, if capital is not made available to sectors which are capable of increasing production and productivity and, above all, if there is no investment in research and development, we can be sure that the rate of expansion of the economy will suffer.

Finally, the mechanism which allocates these capital resources can itself play an important economic role. Even if it tends to distribute capital in accord with the wishes of the public, it may do so only slowly to the accompaniment of the discordant squeaking of its rusty gears. The flexibility and speed of response of our capital allocation mechanism affects directly the adaptability of our productive mechanism, and thereby bears on the long-run prospects of our entire economy.

So far we have considered only the nation's real capital, its machinery, its factories, its goods-in-process, its inventories of raw materials and its final products. But the apportionment of these real resources among industries and individual firms and, indeed, the selection of the physical forms which constitute the embodiment of our capital resources is largely controlled through the funds market— the market on which *money* capital is provided. Thus the allocation process is heavily influenced by the decisions of the nation's financial institutions, its banks, its insurance companies, and a variety of other bodies many of which will come to mind immediately. In addition the government's monetary and fiscal policies obviously play a highly important role in a variety of ways which need not be gone into here. Finally, as we shall see, one may reasonably attribute a regulatory role to the securities markets, and in particular to the markets for stocks and bonds.

The securities markets are characterized by a number of properties which render them specially suitable to serve as capital resource allocators.

First, they offer guidance to business management—information on the current cost of capital which is so important in determining the level of investment which it is appropriate for the firm to undertake. For example, if its stock prices are high so that the company's securities can be exchanged for relatively generous quantities of resources, this is generally taken to indicate that the cost of capital is low and that the net returns to be expected of any given real investment project will be correspondingly generous. Second, the securities markets offer the advantage of accessibility to vast numbers of capitalists, many of whom possess only minuscule amounts of money and yet who in their aggregate have command over vast quantities of wealth. Third, the markets offer a simple mechanism for the transfer of funds that imposes only a minimum of administrative effort upon the lender. Fourth, markets offer him an easily understood evaluation of the financial condition and future prospects of the borrowing firm as indicated by the market price of its securities and by movements in the magnitude of that price. Finally, the market performs an act of magic, for it permits long-term investments to be financed by funds provided by individuals, many of whom wish to make them available for only a very limited period, or who wish to be able to withdraw them at will. Thus it imparts a measure of liquidity to long-term investments that permits their instruments to be sold at a price that yields a lower rate of return than would otherwise be required. In the words of Professor Machlup

The fact that from the point of view of the individual saver it [transfer credit] is only intended to be a short-term loan does not limit the possible ways of using it as much as one might first think. For even though the individual savings are only saved for a temporary period, collectively they may in large part be looked upon as long-term savings of the economic system . . . . The probability that . . . new savings will be sufficient to cover withdrawals of old savings is what makes it possible to invest these short-term funds in production. The system whereby this investment is made through the stock exchange has special advantages, for in this case the transformation of what are short-term credits from the private viewpoint into long-term savings from the social viewpoint can take place to the fullest extent. . . . [1]

For all of these reasons, and no doubt for others as well, one has come to look upon the stock market as the allocator of capital resources *par excellence*, and aside from some uneasiness about the untoward effects of speculation, one is readily inclined toward the view that the stock market constitutes an allocative mechanism of remarkable efficiency.[2] It is a major purpose of this book to probe somewhat more carefully the efficiency of this piece of machinery.

The Stock Exchange as an Illustrative Perfect Market

The stock market is among the subjects which have achieved the status of a textbook cliché. Many such volumes have described this institution as a relatively close approximation to a perfect market, indeed, one of the best which is to be found anywhere in our economy. After all, a hasty glance suggests that it possesses all if not most of the characteristics required of a pure competitive market. Its products are homogeneous: if I buy a share of Republic Steel I don't care which share I happen to get or from whom it happens to have been acquired. Anyone's share of Republic Steel is identical with any other. Also there seem to be many sellers, most of whom are relatively small, though we shall note presently that there are some significant exceptions. Finally,

---

[1] Fritz Machlup, *The Stock Market, Credit and Capital Formation* (London: William Hodge & Company, 1940), p. 225. Reprinted by permission of the publishers.

[2] This is not meant to imply that the bulk of the business sector's new funds are obtained through the stock markets or that a large proportion of the markets' operations help directly to supply new capital. As will be indicated in later chapters, neither of these assertions is true. Firms obtain new funds preponderantly from retained earning, not from new stock issues, and the stock exchanges deal in second-hand shares—not in new issues. As such, the exchanges therefore do not supply new capital. But they can control its allocation by determining the terms (prices) on which funds are available, and by making easily available to investors the alternatives open to them.

the securities markets apparently satisfy the third prime requisite of pure competition, free entry and exit. Anyone who owns a listed security can undertake to sell it and anyone who wishes to acquire one can purchase it. True, entry and exit into the occupations of those who actually operate the market machinery is sometimes restricted. Indeed, in a few cases it is severely limited. It is not easy to become a broker and more difficult to become a floor trader or a specialist. As we shall see, this does have some relevance for the perfection of the market itself. It may mean that the rate of return earned by brokers is somewhat larger than it would have been in the presence of perfect mobility into this occupation. That, in turn, raises the transfer costs incurred in the exchange of securities, and so contributes to the frictions which beset the workings of the market but by itself it need not significantly affect the appropriateness of the stock market as an illustration of pure competition.

One of the first conclusions which the student is expected to draw from the competitive model is that (making suitable allowance for the characteristics of the individual product) on such a market prices tend to be set by the forces of supply and demand at the intersection of the supply and demand schedules. At least at first glance there appears to be no reason to question the applicability of this analysis to the workings of the stock exchange, though I shall presently discuss some of the special features of common stocks which must be borne in mind in applying this model to their pricing. Of course, no one denies the presence of deeper motivations which do not reveal themselves in the elementary supply-demand diagram—for example, the role of anticipations of the future, and of the variety of investment opportunities available to the firm whose security is in question. But in the standard model these underlying determinants exert their influence through their effects on the pertinent supply and demand functions which can then still be taken to determine prices in accord with the ordinary procedures described in our basic competitive analysis.

However, at this point a closer look reveals matters which remain somewhat obscure. Just exactly what are these procedures—the series of events and interrelationships whereby the forces of supply and demand are translated into price quotations? On a real market in the real world one encounters no supply-demand graphs and no one reads off the coordinates of their intersection points. In setting price then, one may well ask exactly who does what to whom—what mechanism translates the disorderly parade of data which serve as a substitute for our neat mathematical functions, into a unique determinate price figure? Here, then, is our first reason for looking more closely at the stock exchange as an illustrative competitive market. This reexamination will indicate the nature of the mechanism which gives effect to the forces of supply and demand. We will find that equilibrium does not simply generate itself and that a very special procedure has been instituted to do the job.

Thus, though this portion of our investigation will reveal few significant departures of the workings of the stock market from those of the purely competitive model, an examination of the relationship between the two can nevertheless prove illuminating. It may offer a somewhat increased understanding of the elaborate arrangements which are required for the operation of the competitive mechanism. More important for our central purposes, having discovered the pricing engine we will be able to discuss the effectiveness of the allocation of capital resources produced by this particular arrangement and whether our conclusions on this subject are a matter of the fortuitous organizational details of the operation of the exchange or whether they may be expected to apply generally to competitive markets.

The Stock Market and the Theory of Resource Allocation

Thus we return to the central topic with which we intend to deal. Granting that the stock exchange constitutes a reasonably close approximation to a competitive market, it seems all the more reasonable to conjecture that it will serve as a relatively effective allocator of resources. However, a bit more thought can lead us to become somewhat suspicious of this conclusion. The reason is the crucial role played by the market value of a company's securities in the entire process. To serve as an effective resource allocator it would appear that the market should value a stock in some manner on the basis of the capitalized value of the company's expected future earnings as determined by the investment opportunities available to it. For it would seem that only if it does so will funds become most readily available to companies which can best make use of them in light of prospective consumer demands, technological circumstances and other pertinent developments in the future. Apparently, only if stocks are valued in this way will funds be provided most abundantly and at most reasonable terms to the most promising innovator who, according to the classical theory of economic development, has the greatest use for them and who is the one that can obtain the profits which will serve as the investor's reward. Finally, it may seem that only if stocks are valued in this way, that is, if they are priced in terms of the prospective earnings of the company, the market can serve as an effective disciplinary device which punishes managements whose operations are inefficient or unprofitable. For only then will poor performance cause the market to deny funds to the company or to provide them only on extremely unfavorable terms.

In sum, the prices assigned to stocks by the free market[3] are critical to the effectiveness of the market as a resource allocator. And if these prices are perversely or even randomly related to future earnings prospects there is no reason to believe that this function will be performed well and effectively. Yet we have all seen cases where the behavior of prices on the stock market has apparently been capricious or even worse, cases where hysteria has magnified largely irrelevant events into controlling influences.[4] Add to this observation a series of extremely careful and sophisticated statistical studies (which will be discussed in Chapter 3) whose evidence is that random elements in stock price behavior are of dominating importance, and we can no longer remain comfortable with the easy assumption that all will work out well in the end. We shall therefore have to inquire into the manner in which stock prices are determined and examine what theory tells us about the likely relationship between prospective earnings and current market values. As may be expected, the results will be far from categorical. We will see some influences which work one way

---

[3] Sometimes special prices are assigned to some shares by the company itself. For example, a firm may offer shares to its current stockholders at prices below those that the stocks would command on the open market. Neoclassical analysis was never meant to be applied to such special arrangements.

[4] This is a phenomenon which does not occur only on the stock market. Similar events have, for example, occurred on the commodity exchanges.

and some the other. But if the discussion does not settle matters it may at least add somewhat to our understanding of the pertinent relationships.

However, even if the stock market proves to provide a good allocative machine, it may somehow turn out that it is not put to good use or that it is largely redundant in that other forces exist which can perform at least some of its allocative functions just as well. As we shall see in the last chapter, not all firms are equally subject to the discipline of the securities markets. In fact we shall observe that a very substantial number of business enterprises in the United States have managed largely to evade this disciplinary mechanism over long periods of time. By comparing the performance of such firms with that of companies over which the market would appear to have exercised a fairly tight continuing control we may be able to form a clearer view of the real role of the market. The statistical problems involved in such an investigation are of course enormous. Yet if the subject is worth studying at all we must, however reluctantly and though only at the end, come to look at the facts: the complex world of reality which constitutes the platonic shadow of our ideal market model.

Chapter Two

The Specialist

OPERATOR OF THE AUTOMATIC MECHANISM

I HAVE BEEN TOLD of some primitive people who, when they first encountered a radio and heard a disembodied voice emerging from its innards, went over to the machine and searched it carefully for the little man concealed within. It is easy for us to be amused by such an unsophisticated exhibition but I shall argue in this chapter that the point of view is not always ill-grounded. The first chapter of this book raised questions about the workings of the supply-demand mechanism, asking precisely how the interaction of supply and demand can actually determine upon an equilibrium value or, for that matter, *any* actual price. In the case of the stock exchange and its determination of the prices of outstanding issues, anyone who is familiar with its workings probably knows the answer. The automatic mechanism simply is not left to run by itself; there *is* a man concealed in the machinery who does really run it. For that, in essence, is one of the major functions of the stock market specialist.

9

The Stock Exchange and the Competitive Model—Preliminary Comments

Before we look a little more closely at the fascinating activities and responsibilities of this individual, it is appropriate to summarize briefly some of the grounds for concern about our understanding of the pricing procedures of the competitive mechanism. It is well known that Walras and Edgeworth expressed some misgivings on this subject in their writings.[1] Walras was perhaps the first to point out that there is no obvious reason to expect identity between the prices yielded by solution of his system of supply-demand equations and the prices which would in fact emerge in a freely competitive market. He therefore developed his theory of tâtonnement in which Walras envisioned a market where people appear with inventories of various goods as well as with well-defined marginal utility functions. His pricing process then begins with someone proposing a set of randomly selected prices. Given these prices, participants in the market next determine upon the amounts which they are prepared to sell and upon the magnitudes of their purchase offers. If, as is to be expected, the initial prices turn out not to clear the market, they are changed. Prices of commodities for which there is an excess demand are increased and those items for which the demand is insufficient are reduced. This process of trial and error pricing and repricing then continues until, according to Walras, the actual market prices converge to those which equate supply and demand. It has been pointed out that a necessary part of this process must be Edgeworth's *recontracting* device. The quantities supplied and demanded at tentative interim prices must themselves constitute only provisional commitments so that if prices change, all bidding—that is, all offers

---

[1] See Leon Walras, *Elements of Pure Economics*, William Jaffé (trans.), (Homewood, Ill.: R. D. Irwin, 1954), pp. 162–3 and 169–72 and various other places throughout the book; F. Y. Edgeworth, *Mathematical Psychics*, London: Kegan Paul & Company, 1881, reproduced as Essay 10 in the series of reprints of Scarce Tracts in Economic and Political Science of The London School of Economics, 1932, p. 35ff and *Papers Relating to Political Economy* (London: Macmillan, 1926, II, pp. 311–12). For a fuller discussion of the Walrasian analysis see Don Patinkin, *Money, Interest and Prices*, Evanston, Ill.: Row, Peterson, 1956, Note B, pp. 377–85.

to buy and sell—can be revised completely.[2] For unless buyers and sellers were permitted to change their minds as prices were modified, the set of prices finally determined by the tâtonnement process would have depended on the nature of the randomly selected initial price bids and the sale and purchase commitments undertaken at these initial prices. People who had already committed themselves and their purchasing power heavily at an earlier stage would not have been able to take advantage of the revised price patterns which emerged out of the process.

I have described the Walras-Edgeworth mechanism only to indicate its artificiality. For we know this is not how things work out in practice. Except, perhaps, in some auction markets people generally do not make tentative bids, nor are prices usually determined by a trial and error process. Such a procedure would be extremely difficult to administer and to keep track of, especially with the large number of participants necessary to render a market competitive in the sense used in economic theory.

The required multiplicity of buyers and sellers itself constitutes one of the major complications which must somehow be handled by a competitive mechanism. Discussions which draw an analogy with an auction involving a small number of bidders only conceal the heroic task constituted by the need to coordinate the purchasing and selling desires of vast numbers of individuals. Just imagine a market composed of thousands of participants and visualize a series of tentative provisional prices and the calculation which would be required in each case to see whether supplies were exactly matched by demands.

In practice, the stock exchange deals with large numbers by operating in a manner somewhat analogous to a representative democracy, and the various bidders make their desires known through a much smaller number of brokers who represent them. This procedure by itself already raises some doubts about the applicability of competitive analysis because where there is only a small number of traders, oligopolistic strategies become possible. One stockholder in

[2] It is not really clear whether Walras fully recognized the role which should have been played by recontracting in his analysis. See Patinkin, *ibid.*, pp. 378–80 and Joseph A. Schumpeter, *History of Economic Analysis* (New York: Oxford University Press, 1954), pp. 1008–9.

a group of 30,000 has no reason to believe he can influence the price of his shares and, accordingly, he is apt to behave like the traditional competitive bidder. But one of a small band of brokers does not always have good grounds for acting in this way.

It is easy to think of other problems encountered in a real market which are not envisioned in the simplest of our theoretical competitive models. For example, at the stock exchange, offers to sell and purchase are not collected up and then confronted simultaneously at some particular moment of the market day. Rather, bids arrive either sporadically or continuously throughout the trading day. Thus pricing becomes a dynamic process in which the time-path of events plays a crucial role. We conclude, then, that supply and demand equations can at best describe only some aspects of the pricing mechanism and that they do not capture some of its significant features—an observation that was emphasized by the neoclassical writers themselves.

The Market's Pricing Solution: The Specialist

The stock exchange has adopted what amounts to a very direct and simple solution of the mechanical problems which have just been discussed. Rather than setting up a subtle mechanism which determines prices automatically it simply appoints someone to do the job. A critical role in the determination of price is effectively delegated to an individual whose decisions are usually final and are apparently rarely questioned. There seems little doubt that, within limits, the price of a stock is adjudicated by the specialist, and that so long as his decision is not wildly unreasonable, price simply is whatever he says the circumstances required. This is amply documented in the recent Securities and Exchange Commission report.[3] For example, the report quotes a discussion between a governor and a specialist in which the latter, referring to a batch of 600 shares which he had supplied at 43 commented,

[3] *Report of Special Study of Securities Markets of the Securities and Exchange Commission*, Part II, 88th Congress, First Session, House Document No. 95, Part 2, July 17, 1963, Washington: U.S. Government Printing Office, 1963. Most of the description of the details of the specialist's operation in this discussion are based on materials drawn from this source.

It could have been sold at any price. I mean, had I wanted to, I could have sold 100 at 43, 100 at $43\frac{1}{4}$, 100 at $43\frac{1}{2}$, 100 at $43\frac{3}{4}$, 100 at $43\frac{7}{8}$, and so on; and just done anything I wanted to. I just didn't. I figured 43 was a very equitable price for the buyers (page 136).

The report goes on to remark (pp. 138–9),

A more dramatic indication of the fact that openings are not mechanical is that the specialist may use discretion in establishing on [*sic*] opening price even though he may have a perfect match between buy and sell market orders. . . . One stock opened on May 29, 1962, off $1\frac{1}{4}$ from the previous day's close, although in this opening the specialist sold 500 shares, indicating that before the opening the specialists had more orders to buy than to sell.[4]

The reader may well wonder whether this discussion does not somewhat exaggerate the power of the specialist. And in a sense it does. For, as we shall see, the market forces do circumscribe his decisions and their disciplinary forces do prevent him being completely arbitrary in his pricing decisions. Nevertheless, the nature of the arrangements is such that he has very considerable discretion in price setting. While it is true, in the last analysis, that he must by and large serve as an interpreter of the supply and demand situation and must set security prices accordingly, we shall see presently that he does not serve simply as an automatic gauge, just reporting on the state of the market—that, in the nature of the case, a great deal must be left to his discretion.

However, I have run ahead of myself. It is well to begin the story at the beginning by explaining for those who are not students of the exchange who the specialist is and what is the nature of his functions.

---

[4] Within the last few months a new set of regulations governing the specialist's activities has been instituted. A portion of the new SEC regulations "along with the companion rules of the New York and American Stock Exchanges . . . contains provisions aimed at preventing specialists from going against the public trend when they open bidding on a stock . . . A specialist would be prohibited from making the first sale of the day at a price inconsistent with the supply and demand picture he had on his order books at the opening of trading.

He could not, for example, open a stock at a price lower than the preceding day's closing if he had more buy than sell orders at that price." *New York Times*, September 25, 1964, pp. 1, 61.

The Operations of the Specialist

Each security dealt with on the New York Stock Exchange (and on other stock exchanges in the United States) is handled by one or more specialists. The specialist's basic function is to bring buyers and sellers together. When someone wishes to purchase a security, it is the specialist's job to provide a seller to supply his needs at some appropriate price and, similarly, it is up to him to arrange for the purchase of securities which people desire to sell. Many of these buy and sell orders indicate proposed buying and selling prices ("I will purchase fifty shares at any price no higher than $14\frac{7}{8}$") and, as we shall see, this complicates the supply-demand equilibrating functions of the specialist. It should also be recognized that some securities are exchanged without the help of a specialist, but usually the terms of such trades which take place outside the organized exchanges follow closely the prices for similar stocks traded through the agency of the specialist.

All specialists are members of the exchange and, as an indication of the numbers involved, we note that in the middle of 1962 there were 360 specialists registered on the New York Stock Exchange, all of whom were drawn from among its total membership of 1,366. On the American Stock Exchange there were 159 specialists among its total membership of 499. Since some 1,100 stocks are listed on the New York Stock Exchange, on the average each specialist there deals in about three different securities. Some securities, particularly those whose volume is especially heavy, are handled by several competing specialists. According to the SEC report there are now only thirty-seven stocks traded by competing specialists and the number of stocks handled in this way had been declining continually and rather rapidly.

To become a specialist a member of the exchange must make formal application to the exchange and receive its approval. Before approval is granted, he must satisfy the exchange that he possesses the ability to perform the job and he must agree to abide by the rules under which the specialist's activities are conducted. He is also required to show that he can meet the capital requirements prescribed by the exchange. According to the SEC report (p. 69), the current capital requirement is fairly low and generally considered to be only nominal because most specialists possess funds which exceed the required minimum. In any event, it has been suggested that the present capital requirement is highly inadequate and it is under review.[5]

The specialist has two basic sources of income, brokerage fees and the profits derived from his trading transactions. Before we can understand how these earnings arise we must inquire a little more closely into his mode of operation. As has been stated, it is one of the specialist's duties to see that stocks which are offered for sale (at a price which is acceptable in a sense to be described presently) are indeed sold and that all (acceptably priced) demands for stocks are also satisfied. Since only by the sheerest coincidence will candidate sellers and purchasers appear on the market at precisely the same moment in evenly matched groups (quantity supplied equals quantity demanded at presently quoted price), the specialist can only satisfy this obligation by standing ready to buy or sell some of this stock himself. If at any point there is an excess supply of the security (quantity supplied greater than quantity demanded) he is normally expected to purchase it for his own account and, except in unusual circumstances, when there is an excess demand he must provide the security from his inventory. The process will be described presently and in some detail with the aid of specific numerical illustrations. We may then distinguish explicitly between the specialist's *brokerage* function—his role as an intermediary between buyer and seller—as the man who carries out the transfer of their securities—and his performance as a *dealer for his own account* in meeting his obligation to supply securities, or a customer for securities, when the market desires them.

The commitment to act as residual buyer or seller is a demanding undertaking and, in principle, it can be the source of substantial profits or losses. One might surmise that if the magnitudes and timing of his purchases and sales were the resultants of his completely

---

[5] Under the new regulations (which were announced recently) the specialists' capital requirements have been increased substantially (on the N.Y. Stock Exchange to a minimum sufficient to permit the holding of a 1,200 share inventory of each stock he handles). Nevertheless, it was reported that no more than four specialist firms would find it necessary to post additional funds. *New York Times, ibid.,* p. 61. Indeed, for most stocks the new capital requirement may still be considered minuscule.

passive response to events on the market, over the long run his profits and losses would, on the average, cancel out, since as far as he was concerned whether he was buying or selling at any particular moment would appear to be determined randomly.[6] One might expect, therefore, that the bulk of the specialist's income would be derived from his brokerage function, the fee he receives in his role as executor of orders for other brokers on the exchange who are not themselves specialists.

These guesses turn out to be wrong. While brokerage commissions do provide a substantial proportion of the specialists' income, trading profits are by no means negligible and in some years, for example in 1959, they constituted more than half of specialists' incomes. A number of specialist units (firms) realize as much as eighty percent of their remuneration from trading profits and the larger the size of the specialist unit the larger, in general, is the proportion of its income which is derived from trading profits. In addition, a sample study indicates that the vast majority of the specialists' trading transactions turn out to be profitable. An analysis of twenty-five stocks over a three-week period indicated that over eighty-seven percent of stocks in the cases examined were purchased at a price below that at which the specialist had previously sold them in his previous transaction or were sold at prices above those corresponding to his preceding purchase.[7]

We must conclude our description of the functions of the specialist by mentioning another task which he is usually expected to perform.

[6] Actually one might even expect him to come out on the short end. If a preponderance of private traders usually bought stocks when it was profitable to buy and sold them when selling was lucrative, the specialist, as residual buyer or seller would be forced into the opposite timing pattern, which would presumably be rather unprofitable. The profitability of the specialists' trading operations may, then, perhaps be ascribed in part to poor management by other traders.

[7] SEC *Report*, p. 83. It should be noted, however, that these figures do not indicate whether these specialists had been holding their own in comparison with the market as a whole. That is, they may have sustained an "opportunity loss" in the sense that they might have done better, e.g., simply by investing their money in stocks and holding on to them for the period in question.

It has been argued that the profitability of the specialists' trading operations shows that stock-market price movements are not really random in character as many statisticians allege. This "random-walk" hypothesis is discussed in some detail in the following chapter.

As put by the New York Stock Exchange pamphlet, *Now, About the Specialist . . . ,*

> He must maintain, insofar as reasonably practicable, fair and orderly markets in the stocks which he services. When there is temporary disparity between supply and demand he buys or sells for his own account to narrow the price changes between sales. By doing this, he keeps price continuity more orderly than would otherwise be the case. . . (p. 3).

In other words, the specialist is expected to contribute a stabilizing influence to market prices and this is emphasized heavily in the public relations literature on the stock market. In discussions of this function readers are frequently reminded of the valiant efforts of the specialist during various (minor) stock market crises to stem unruly price movements. We shall return presently to a closer look at this assignment and examine whether the nature of the specialist's operations and the built-in motivating mechanism which directs his activities is such as to make for successful stabilization.

From the preceding discussion we see, then, that a principal function of the specialist is the execution of the orders placed with him by other members of the exchange. He must arrange for the sales and purchases desired by investors in securities. And as part of that operation he must often serve as the judge of the price at which orders are executed.

Let us now examine more closely the extent of the specialist's influence over this price.

Types of Specialists' Orders and His Price-Setting Discretion

To see what permits the specialist some degree of discretion in his pricing decision and enables him thereby to influence the profitability of his transactions it is necessary to examine the several types of order which the specialist's customers can place with him.

One of the basic types of transaction is the *market order* in which the customer asks the specialist to make a sale or a purchase at the current market price. Though this arrangement may seem quite explicit in its instructions, in practice it offers the specialist a range of choice. When several such orders arrive simultaneously the balance between supply and demand will usually be changed thereby, and so the price previously quoted need no longer be appropriate. It is then up to the specialist to determine the level of the current market price —the terms of execution of the market orders. If the market for the security in question happens to be thin (if trading in the security is inactive), time gaps will, typically, separate transactions and the last preceding transaction will then serve only as a very imperfect guide for the setting of current price so that the specialist must, once again, use his judgment to set price.[8]

The specialist is offered even more discretion by a second type of transaction, the so-called *not-held order*, an arrangement which should be mentioned even though it probably constitutes a very minor portion of specialists' operations. Such an order is defined by the exchange as a request either to buy or to sell a stock in which the broker "*is relieved of all responsibilities* with respect to the time of execution and the price or prices of execution."[9] By placing a not-held order, a customer, then, explicitly asks the specialist to use his own judgment—to do the best he can in securing favorable terms for the transaction.[10]

Finally we come to a variety of transaction which is perhaps the most important component in the specialist's operations, the *limit order:* an order to sell at any price above x dollars or to purchase at any price of y dollars or less. Upon receipt, a limited order is entered by the specialist into his "book." The book thus contains a record of all buy and sell orders which have been entrusted to him for

[8] A stock exchange regulation does prohibit the specialist from purchasing for his own account so long as he holds any unexecuted market order to buy, and imposes a similar limitation on his sales.

[9] New York Stock Exchange, Department of Floor Procedure, "Dealings in Stocks," 1958, p. 41. (Italics in original.)

[10] Because a not-held order is subject to a variety of abuses involving the specialist's use of his inside information about supplies and demands to gain an advantage for persons in whose welfare he may have some interest, in 1952 some attempt was made to limit its use. On first reading this regulation seems to constitute a ban on the acceptance of not-held orders by specialists, but in practice that ban has apparently been ineffective and a number of specialists have continued to participate in operations of this sort though they have perhaps used considerable discretion and have done so only in very special cases. However, I have been given to understand that the ban on acceptance of not-held orders by the specialist has recently begun to be enforced.

execution but which under their terms cannot be carried out at the current market price. If the market price changes so that several bids become eligible for execution simultaneously, for example, if the price falls to 30 and several customers have indicated their willingness to buy at that price, then the order first received by the specialist at that price will normally be executed first.

The specialist's book is very clearly a rich mine of information though it does represent a rather limited and, perhaps, a somewhat biased sample. In effect, it makes him the sole repository of something approximating supply and demand schedules for the security which he handles. One might well expect that with possession of this sort of inside information and some skill and experience, it should not be too difficult for him to learn how transactions can be made to yield profits.[11]

The confrontation of limit orders in the book seems to resemble closely the classic supply-demand price determination process. Yet even this sort of order leaves to the specialist some degree of price-setting discretion.

An example should make the process clear. Suppose at some point

[11] It may be mentioned as a *curiosum* that the information contained in the book is not always interpreted in the manner in which one might expect. According to the SEC report "Some specialists testified that the trend of the market is indicated by the orders on the book—that a book which contains many sell orders is characteristic of a stock which will increase in price, while a book containing many buy orders indicates that the price will decline" (*op. cit.*, p. 76). This interpretation, of course, conflicts with the more straightforward view that an excess of supply orders will lead to price declines and an excess of purchase orders will cause prices to rise. The somewhat subtle explanation offered for the less unorthodox reading is a matter of expectations. It maintains that limit orders are placed predominately by more knowledgeable investors who will propose to sell above the current market price when they expect market price to rise and offer to buy below current price when they anticipate a price fall. Interpreted in this way, the book serves as a sort of opinion poll of people who are in the know rather than a straightforward report on static supply-demand functions. Which interpretation in fact better approximates the truth can only be determined by statistical analysis. Unfortunately, the specialists' book is kept in such a way that it is very difficult to determine what was actually on its pages at any particular moment in the past. Some types of orders are cancelled automatically at the end of the day of entry while others are cancelled only as they are executed or withdrawn by the customer.

the specialist's book contains the orders summarized in Table 1 at the prices indicated: column 2 shows that he holds an order for 200 shares

TABLE 1. ORDERS IN A HYPOTHETICAL SPECIALIST'S BOOK

Price (1)	Buy Orders (2)	Total Demanded (3)	Sell Orders (4)	Total Supplied (5)	Excess Demand (6)
40	200	300	0	0	300
$40\frac{1}{8}$	100	100	0	0	100
$40\frac{1}{4}$	0	0	100	100	−100
$40\frac{3}{8}$	0	0	200	300	−300

to be purchased at any price no higher than 40, and 100 to be bought at a price not exceeding $40\frac{1}{8}$. Thus (third column) the total amount demanded at a price of 40 is 300 shares, while at $40\frac{1}{8}$ only 100 shares will be demanded, etc. The supply relationships in the next two columns are explained similarly. In a market in which no specialist were present, supply and demand would clearly dictate a price somewhere between $40\frac{1}{8}$ and $40\frac{1}{4}$. But with price not permitted to vary by an amount smaller than $\frac{1}{8}$, in the situation represented in the table there exists no price at which the market will clear by itself. The specialist must then purchase or sell for his own account to balance supply and demand. But then he can set price anywhere between 40 and $40\frac{3}{8}$ if only he is willing to offset the resultant excess demand or supply by trading for his own account. He can open at 40 if he is willing to supply 300 shares, at $40\frac{1}{8}$ if he is prepared to offer 100 shares at that price, etc.

TABLE 2. ORDERS IN A HYPOTHETICAL BOOK

Price	Buy Orders	Sell Orders
40	100	0
41	0	100

Moreover, there are other profit and price setting opportunities which the limit order makes available to the specialist. Suppose that at some point during the day his book contains only the orders shown in Table 2. Clearly no trading is then possible since the demand price is lower than the supply price. Now, the specialist is not permitted to "undercut" for his own account any pair of executable orders (if there were 100 shares offered at 40 and 100 demanded at 41 he would have had to execute the two orders at some intermediate price without purchasing or selling any of the amount for himself). But with supplies and demands as shown in Table 2 the specialist can enter the market without interfering with any executable transactions. He will normally set bid and asked prices in between those shown in his book. Say, he may let it be known that he stands ready to buy at $40\frac{1}{8}$ and to sell at $40\frac{3}{8}$. If subsequently buyers and sellers appear and take advantage of his offer he will make a profit of $\frac{1}{4}$ of a point on each security bought and then sold by him. Moreover, his book offers him a degree of protection in this process, for if, for example, many sellers were to offer him shares at his bid price of $40\frac{1}{8}$ but no buyers were to show up, he could (in addition to reducing his purchase offer price) dispose of at least some of the shares he did not want by selling them to the potential purchaser whose order appears on the book, i.e., he could dispose of as many as 100 shares at 40.

A final relevant situation is that where a buying price is above some selling price in the book so that a sale is possible. It is then up to the specialist to decide on the intermediate price at which the transaction should be executed. When the spread between buying and selling limit prices is very large, as can happen on thin markets, particularly at the opening of trading, the specialist's latitude in price determination is correspondingly wide—though there are rules which are designed to limit it somewhat.

The preceding examples should have suggested the extent of the price-setting freedom permitted the specialist by the limit order and the degree of control which he exercises over the profitability of his transactions. Let us now consider in theoretical terms some of the implications of these arrangements.

The Specialist as a Competitive Price Setter

In a competitive market, price is in equilibrium (whether stable or unstable) if and only if it yields neither excess supply nor excess demand. Now, under the terms of operation of the specialist system there is a sense in which the market price must almost always constitute an equilibrium value. Since the specialist is normally required by his assignment to "make a market" at the current price, every one who wishes to sell at the current price must be able to do so and every one who wishes to purchase must be able to find the securities he desires. Then, necessarily, price must always be such that the sum of excess demands *including the specialist's own excess demand on his account* is always zero. How, then, can it be suggested that the specialist may arrive at pricing decisions other than those corresponding to a competitive equilibrium?

The answer, simply, is that the specialist must be treated not as a competitor but, on the contrary (at least for a narrow "normal" price range) as a price administering monopolist or oligopolist. In making this assertion I must emphasize that it is meant neither to be critical nor to imply impropriety of any sort. It is intended merely to describe the facts of the matter and to indicate the sorts of analytic devices which can appropriately be used to describe the situation. Nor does it pretend to depart significantly from the spirit of the neoclassical analysis, the inappropriateness of whose supply-demand apparatus to short-run price determination was clearly recognized, for example, by Marshall.

In this light we must reinterpret the statement that on the securities market excess demands, including both those of the market and of the specialist himself, will normally approach zero. In a graphic representation corresponding to this assertion, it would not be legitimate to construct an excess demand curve for the market simply by adding together the demand curves of the specialist and those of other participants in the market. A demand or offer curve is not relevant for the operations of the specialist any more than a supply curve is pertinent to the workings of the monopolist. A demand curve, after all, reports how much the person or group in question would be willing to buy at different alternative *fixed* prices. But as far as the specialist is concerned the price is not pre-determined. He is not faced by a price datum to which he must adjust his actions; rather he can influence and, within limits, even determine that price for himself. In terms of the example of Table 1, he is confronted by the alternative price-quantity options given by the market's excess demand function (columns 1 and 6 in Table 1) and his strategic stance will ultimately determine which of these he selects.

Thus if the specialist operates in the spirit of the profit system, that is, if he pursues his economic self-interest, all the classical analysis of the equilibrium in a market in which one monopolist faces a group of competitors should apply here. The equilibrium point should not occur at the intersection of the offer curve of the specialist with the corresponding offer curve of the other participants. Rather, the specialist should choose to end up at the spot which is most favorable to him from among all the points that constitute the market's offer curve.

In terms of the Edgeworth box diagram which we are discussing, he should end up at the point of tangency between the market's offer curve and one of his indifference curves (or at the nearest approximation to that point from among the finite number of points representing the market's current trading offers). Such an equilibrium point will not normally lie on the contract locus and so, unlike a competitive equilibrium solution, the outcome will not be Pareto optimal; that is, it will be socially undesirable in that it wastes opportunities to improve things for everyone concerned. The prices arrived at on the securities markets and the quantities of securities sold and purchased are then not socially optimal because some other price levels and some other quantities could be chosen in a way which was advantageous to some participants and disadvantageous to none.

Nor is there any reason to think that things will be materially different where several specialists compete for the sale or purchase of a given security. Even in the case of the few stocks which are handled by several competing specialists there is reason to believe that competition is not effective. According to the SEC report (pp. 62–3) "The commission firms do not shop for the best service but often give each competitor half their brokerage business." And even if competition were more effective, it would be of an oligopolistic variety.

Unfortunately, there appears to be no empirical test which will show whether specialists behave in practice more like competitors or monopolists.[12] We cannot determine whether a specialist has or has not

[12] That is, whether they determine their purchases in accord with an independently established demand schedule one of whose variables is price, or whether they "administer" prices in a manner which promotes their profit.

settled on a competitive price because we cannot observe his offer (demand) curve. Nor can we use as a criterion the clearing of the market for, as we have seen, in terms of what can be observed the market will always be cleared. Yet, despite the fact that nothing can be proved or perhaps because of it, and because the specialist himself will normally be unable to judge whether his behavior is "truly competitive" I am inclined to suspect strongly that the specialist's decisions tend to depart rather unrandomly from the competitive ideal. The predominant profitability of his transactions would seem to accord with this surmise, though we shall see presently that other interpretations are also possible. After all, in circumstances so vaguely defined and so difficult to judge, it is the easiest thing in the world for a man to convince himself that what is good for himself is also good for the market's other participants, so long as his acts are neither obviously unethical nor patently harmful to anyone. It is common enough for persons to confuse their own interests with the requisites of public virtue.

I shall argue presently that it would really be quite unreasonable of us to expect the specialist to behave otherwise. We cannot really ask a man to act as though he were a pure competitor when he is not, especially where there are no indices which can inform him whether he has satisfied the requirements of competitive behavior. And in an economic system whose regulatory mechanism is based largely on the pursuit of self interest we cannot reasonably demand of a few individuals that they order their behavior on totally different principles. But let me postpone this subject for the moment and turn to the second major charge which is placed upon the specialist, his guardianship of the market's "orderliness."

The Specialist as Stabilizer

Though the specialist is clearly enjoined to act in a manner which increases the stability of market prices, the meaning of this assignment is not perfectly obvious, and a number of different tasks have been included under that heading. For example, it is generally agreed that during temporary crises he is supposed to try to stem the tide. When the market price of a security begins to drop very sharply, he should, presumably, either stand ready to purchase amounts sufficient to reduce significantly the magnitude of the price fall or he should arrange for a suspension of all trading. But the specialist's responsibility is generally taken to extend beyond the relatively rare temporary crises. It is often also held to be part of his task to reduce the magnitude of the price variations which occur in the course of ordinary day-to-day market operations. It is suggested that in a market situation where price would have risen by, say, three points, the specialist's presence should serve to reduce the magnitude of that increase.

Before discussing this obligation, it is well to point out that there is one stabilization task definitely not considered part of the specialist's assignment. It is generally agreed that the specialist cannot be expected to do much about long-term price movements. No one man nor any one firm can be expected to continue purchasing day after day as price continues to fall, or to sell without limit as price continues to rise. For no group's inventory of securities and no individual's capital can last long before such a protracted onslaught. It is beside the present point to criticize the relatively small amount of capital required of the specialist by Exchange regulations because, no matter how stringent these requirements were to become, they would only enable the specialist to deal more effectively with temporary price movements.

But let us return to the day-by-day stabilization process and the view that the specialist should at all times act in a manner which serves to reduce the magnitude of price variations. This is apparently the position taken by the SEC investigating group. Their test of the success of the specialist's performance as a stabilizer seems only to make sense on such an interpretation.

There is one important respect in which the specialist does dampen short-run oscillations and does so automatically in the course of his work. By providing a continuous market for a security whose trading is thin the specialist eliminates the wide short-term price swings which would otherwise accompany almost every transaction. In such a market a seller's appearance rarely coincides with that of a buyer whose purchase desires match his offerings. If he is unwilling to delay his sale indefinitely, a seller may then be able to find a purchaser for his stocks only with the aid of a comparatively substantial reduction in price. A thin market would therefore characteristically exhibit wide price swings with market values falling abruptly each time some stocks were offered for sale and rising sharply each time someone desired to make a purchase. By providing a continuous source of supply and a continuous demand the specialist materially reduces this sort of oscillation.

But, apparently, the specialist's obligation to maintain an orderly market requires more of him than this. He is, in effect, expected to time his purchases and sales in a way which is designed to reduce the amplitude of fluctuations. For example, it is suggested that he should purchase when market prices have been falling and sell when market price has been rising. This is precisely the spirit of the new SEC regulations affecting the activities of floor traders which impose on them the obligation to make certain that 75 percent or more of their transactions are stabilizing in this particular sense.[13]

Unfortunately, most of the conclusions of the study on this subject must be rejected as naïve and superficial. Engineers have long known that the design of stabilization mechanisms is a tricky business which can very easily backfire. A mechanism which, on common sense considerations, would appear to be highly stabilizing can, in fact, increase the frequency and amplitude of fluctuations if there is any slight miscalculation in its design. Similar results have recently been demonstrated in discussions of income and employment stabilization.[14]

An effective stabilizing procedure must plan carefully the timing and magnitude of its actions. It must take into account not only the current values of its target variables but also their rates of change.

[13] The *Wall Street Journal*, Wednesday, June 3, 1964, p. 4. Moreover, the long discussion of stabilization and stabilization tests in the special study of the SEC (p. 96 ff) concerns itself with this type of stabilization activity. The bulk of those pages is devoted to an examination of alternative tests of specialists' performance designed to determine whether it was or was not stabilizing in the sense we are discussing.

[14] See Milton Friedman, "The Effects of a Full-Employment Policy on Economic Stability: A Formal Analysis," *Essays in Positive Economics* (Chicago: University of Chicago Press, 1953); A. W. Phillips, "Stabilization Policy in a Closed Economy," *Economic Journal*, 64 (June, 1954); and W. J. Baumol, "Pitfalls in Contracyclical Policies: Some Tools and Results," *The Review of Economics and Statistics*, 43 (February, 1961).

To reduce the amplitude and frequency of price fluctuations it is not enough simply to add to sales when market price is relatively high and to purchase when it is comparatively low. For example, increased sales at a high price which are undertaken just after the peak of a cycle is passed may only serve to accelerate the downturn, so that this type of measure may actually serve only to increase the frequency and amplitude of fluctuations beyond what they would have been in the absence of intervention.

In short, stabilization policy is a dangerous game for amateurs and I include in this category many people whose expertise in the operations of the fields into which they are trying to introduce stability is clearly beyond question. If, as has been shown, a policy in which the government increases its expenditure beyond what it would otherwise have been whenever income is falling and reduces its outlays (relatively) whenever income is rising can easily aggravate fluctuations, there is little reason to believe that *ad hoc* devices analogously circum-scribing the specialists' activities will not have similar results. It is easy to construct a model which fully illustrates these dangers and the likelihood that they will be encountered in practice.

There is one group of economists which goes to the opposite extreme and suggests that any stabilizing admonitions to the specialist are likely to be supererogatory. This is the optimistic position taken by members of the "Chicago school," in the belief that specialists need only look after their own profits and stabilization will thereby be taken care of automatically. Their argument is that anyone who makes profits on a fluctuating market must sell at a high price and buy at a low price and that this is all that is required for stabilization. The weakness of this line of reasoning has just been indicated and I believe it has been amply demonstrated elsewhere.[15] Nevertheless, while continuing to reject this simplistic view of a difficult problem I do have very severe doubts about the desirability of regulations which undertake to require stabilizing behavior of the specialist. It is inappropriate to impose upon the specialist a task which no one knows how to carry out. If procedures which have been designed and

[15] See my "Speculation, Profitability, and Stability," *Review of Economics and Statistics*, 39 (August, 1957), and Murray C. Kemp, "Speculation, Profitability, and Price Stability," *ibid.*, 45 (May, 1963).

tested by methods no more rigorous than the exercise of common sense can easily make things worse, then simple discretion would seem to dictate that we leave the specialist to concern himself exclusively with his other tasks.

The preceding comment is, however, not meant to rule out the possibility that the specialist can play an important stabilizing role in cushioning sharp but transitory price movements. It has been claimed (on grounds which have not been clearly specified) that during the scare following President Eisenhower's heart attack, the specialist kept the resulting fall in stock prices to about one-half what it would otherwise have been. I will now argue that stabilizing behavior of this variety may also serve the specialist's interests and need not be the consequence only of devotion to duty. Even the assertion that the price fall was kept to *one-half* its maximal amount can be rationalized in this manner—for, as I shall show, a crude attempt at profit maximization might well have led the specialist to keep the price fall to just that figure.

Suppose, then, that as the result of a temporary shock the price of some security falls but that our specialist expects it to return soon to its initial level, P_i, at which he hopes to dispose of whatever additional holdings he acquires during the period in question. Let the (lower) equilibrium price be P_e, at which the market would clear without the intervention of the specialist. Suppose, moreover, that as an approximation, he assumes the supply curve of securities to him (the market's excess supply function) to be linear, that it is, in fact, the straight line, SS', in Figure 1. If, say, the specialist were to elect to support the security's price at level OP, he would have to purchase OE shares (the market's excess supply at that price), which he would subsequently resell at price OP$_i$. His total profit on the transaction would then have been OE (OP$_i$−OP) which is represented by the shaded area PABP$_i$. To maximize his profit he must select that support price intermediate between P_e and P_i which renders the corresponding rectangle as large as possible. A standard geometric result[16]

[16] This result is also obtained by treating P$_i$P$_i$' as the specialist's marginal (and average) revenue curve, and SS' as his average cost curve. By standard construction the corresponding (linear) marginal cost and revenue curves must intersect at B', the midpoint of segment P$_i$R.

tells us that this maximal rectangle (the largest rectangle which can be inscribed within right triangle P_eRP_i) will have a corner at A′, the midpoint of line segment P_eR, and will correspond to a support price level equal to[17] $\frac{1}{2}(P_i+P_e)$. The specialist will have maximized his

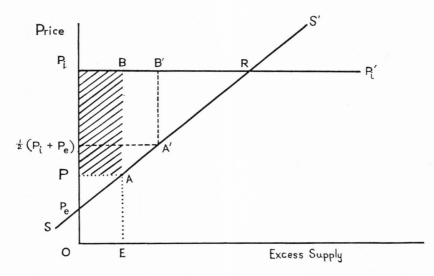

FIGURE 1

[17] A rudimentary proof utilizing the differential calculus is easily constructed. The supply function may be written $S = a + bP$, where P is the price offered by the specialist, and S is the number of shares then sold to him. His expected profit from the transaction, when he finally does sell these securities at price P_i is

$$\Pi = (P_i - P)S = (P_i - P)(a + bP) = aP_i + bP_iP - aP - bP^2.$$

His profit will then be at a maximum when

$$\frac{d\Pi}{dP} = bP_i - a - 2bP = 0$$

or

(1) $$P = \frac{P_i - (a/b)}{2}$$

To interpret this result we must first evaluate the equilibrium price, P_e, in terms of the linear supply function. At the market equilibrium price there must be no excess supply so that we will have $S = 0$, i.e., $a + bP_e = 0$, so that $P_e = -a/b$. Thus, by (1) the profit maximizing price for the specialist is

$$P = (P_i + P_e)/2$$

as was to be shown.

expected profit by supporting price at a level half way between the initial price, P_i, and the price level, P_e, to which the security would have fallen in the absence of his intervention!

What is the real significance of this result? It is surely not in the curious coincidence between the occurrence of the $\frac{1}{2}$ figure in the expression for the profit maximizing price and the appearance of the same number in the public relations releases. One cannot help suspecting that the figure in the popular lore very likely represents no more than a crude quantification of a vague intuitive impression, and it is also difficult to give credence to the assumption that specialists effectively approximate maximum profits even implicitly and sub-consciously, in accord with a linearity assumption. We must, there-fore, regretfully conclude that the identity of the two figures, though perhaps amusing, is coincidental and without significance. The note-worthy implication of our result is its demonstration that pursuit of self-interest can in some circumstances make an effective stabilizer of the specialist.

However, a very similar model can be used to show that things will not always work out in this way. For consider the case where the market's excess supply function is non-linear in a rather extreme though by no means implausible manner, that during a crisis almost every potential investor's demand price falls to a roughly similar level. That is, I assume here that no purchasers stand ready to buy at any price above the low market clearing price P_e, which serves as a short-run panic equilibrium price. In that case it is in the specialist's interest to acquire the available unwanted supply of securities for himself at as low a price as possible, specifically, at a price only slightly above that at which other purchasers would be willing to enter the market. Here, self-interest on the part of the specialist would therefore lead to little cushioning of the fall in market price.

We may now summarize the results of this section. It has been seen that the specialist's stabilization function might conceivably be taken to encompass four quite different tasks:

1. reduction in the magnitude of long-term price trends;
2. reduction in the magnitude of very short-term oscillations resulting from the discontinuous flow of supplies and demands (in thin markets);

3. reduction in the amplitude and frequency of other price fluctuations of moderate amplitude;

4. reduction in the magnitude of sudden price moves which constitute temporary crises.

We have seen that no one does or reasonably could expect the specialist to do much about the first of these. The second function he performs automatically when he carries out his obligation to "make a market." The third task is one on which we are rather thoroughly in the dark, because no one really knows what does and what does not effectively dampen these fluctuations. And, finally, we concluded that to the extent the specialist is driven by self-interest, he may sometimes play his role as a stabilizer during temporary crises weakly and erratically.[18] Assuming that stabilization in any or all of these senses is desirable—something which is not always as self-evident as it may at first appear (cf. note 21, below)—we must ask what change in behavior (if any) it is reasonable to demand of the specialist.

The Specialist and the Profit Motive

It is sometimes forgotten that Adam Smith ended his famous invisible hand passage with the observation, at once delightful and profound, that he had

. . . never known much good done by those who affected to trade for the public good. It is an affectation, indeed, not very common among merchants, and very few words need be employed in dissuading them from it.

Much of the rationale of our profit system lies imbedded in this statement. That system operates effectively and satisfactorily so long as our economy is organized in a manner such that the pursuit of

---

[18] "The S.E.C. found that some specialists in two major breaks—the sell-off of May, 1962, and the panic that rode on the heels of the assassination last November—either walked away from the market, or accelerated the decline by throwing large quantities of stock at the tape." *New York Times*, September 27, 1964, section 3, p. 1. The recent regulation changes are designed to prevent this sort of behavior, and reaffirm strongly the specialist's obligation " . . . to assist in the maintenance, so far as practicable, of a fair and orderly market. . . . "

self-interest by individuals (within the set rules) is also likely to lead automatically to maximum social welfare or at least to a closer approximation thereto than would be attained by any available pattern of intervention. Where the arrangements are imperfect in this respect, it is unreasonable to expect that some individuals will act contrary to their own interests in order to promote public well being. Indeed, as an individualist I am uneasy about the consequences when the individual businessman takes it upon himself to decide what should be done for *my* welfare. I believe, then, that the specialist who pursues his own interests should not be subjected to censure for doing so. If the results of his acts do not appear to be entirely beneficial to society it is hardly appropriate for us to deal with the problem by lecturing the specialist on his public responsibility and expecting him to be the rare member of our economy whose role requires him to sacrifice his own well-being for that of others. Rather one should, if appropriate, change the rules of the game so that the invisible hand does indeed direct his activity in such a manner that "by pursuing his own interest he . . . promotes that of the society. . . . "

I am not necessarily arguing that such changes are currently required. My purpose in this chapter has been to show that the stock market's competitive mechanism is by no means completely automatic and to describe some of the activities of the person who really drives the machine.[19] In doing so it has been necessary to draw attention to matters which to some observers may constitute grounds for criticism. My concluding comments have only suggested the terms in which such criticisms might appropriately be cast.

Summary comment

The central observation of this chapter, that it does take a group of persons to operate the pricing process, does not argue that this process is non-competitive. As a matter of fact, I believe that, despite the consequences of the presence of only small numbers of brokers

---

[19] Note that in the over-the-counter market there are often a number of firms who make the market for any one security. Hence, for this market, the theory of oligopoly would presumably be more appropriate than it is in the case of the stock exchanges where a single specialist frequently makes the market for a given stock.

and specialists,[20] the market does approximate relatively closely the short-run competitive equilibrium process. Rather, we may conclude that *any* such equilibrating process is likely to need a little help of the sort provided by the specialist.

But though the market may yield something very much akin to a short-run competitive solution, we shall see in the next chapter that there is far less reason to expect it to approach a long-run competitive equilibrium. Moreover, the consequences of this observation constitute no mere technicality. They can have most serious implications for the allocation of society's capital resources, as we shall see.[21]

[20] The monopolistic elements introduced by the small number of brokers and specialists may perhaps merely be expected to increase the magnitude of transactions costs rather than interfering more profoundly with the workings of the market. It is as though a competitive industry were to obtain one of its inputs (the specialists' services) from a noncompetitive supplier. This would clearly not imply that the user of these inputs was operating noncompetitively. In this connection one reader supplied the following interesting comment:
"The commission structure is an interesting aspect of monopoly pricing. The greatest sin a member firm can commit—and one for which they will lose their membership in the cartel—is to give a rebate to a customer. The exchange sends out auditors on a regular basis and they check the member firms exclusively for this. Obviously there are a host of side payments that are given to attract customers—research reports, direct wires, dinners, 'hot' new issues, etc. But the commission structure itself is firm. New firms have therefore arisen to take advantage of the spread . . . that trade listed stocks at a lower commission structure. The exchange of course . . . wants the third market regulated too and preferably regulated out of business. But these firms just sell price—no research reports. Moreover the commission structure surely rivals steel rates as the prime example of a fixed price: the structure has changed, we believe, only three times in over a hundred years."
[21] Since this chapter was written, I have come across a significant article dealing with aspects of the same subject: George J. Stigler's "Public Regulation of the Securities Markets," *Journal of Business*, 37 (April 1964). In this paper Stigler deals with the specialist's role in facilitating transactions on a market where the balancing of supply and demand occupies a substantial period of time. He develops an extremely interesting model in which demands and supplies are simulated by sequences of randomly selected numbers and shows what sorts of price variation might be expected to result. He also describes the types of time-path which might be expected if there were a change in the underlying equilibrium value of the price variable and argues, convincingly, that it would be most undesirable for the specialist to reduce the magnitude of all price movements and

thereby decrease the speed of adjustment toward the new equilibrium price. This position certainly seems to be valid. However, it does conceal some difficulties which may mislead the unwary. The main problem lies in the determination and definition of "equilibrium." In using this term, does Stigler refer to long-run equilibrium price, and if so, how does one determine what it is? Where demand falls sharply but temporarily it can be maintained that for a brief period the equilibrium price is one which is well below that which prevailed before the news was received. But surely it is not the specialist's obligation to hasten movements toward that lower price level!

There are many other interesting ideas in Stigler's article, among them the suggestion that inventory and queuing theory may be of some help in determining how effective the specialist has been in providing a continuous market. To be specific, given the nature of the risks and holding costs, the optimal amounts of cash and the number of securities which it is desirable for a specialist to have in his possession at different times should, at least in principle, be determinable with the aid of these types of analysis. This is so since the most felicitous quantities of cash and securities must constitute the optimal inventories of these items.

Chapter Three

True Value Will Out

SECURITY PRICES AND LONG-RUN COMPETITIVE

EQUILIBRIUM

IT SEEMS GENERALLY AGREED that the price of a company's shares should, ideally, measure the value of the firm whose ownership they represent. More specifically, most analysts would doubtless agree that the price of a security should be determined, ultimately, by the prospective earnings of the company.[1] It is not clear, however, how

---

[1] Though as we shall see, the respective roles of earnings and dividends in this process are sometimes disputed. There is plausibility in the position that the stockholder is ultimately interested in what he himself receives, that is, he is therefore concerned immediately with his dividend receipts rather than with company earnings, except insofar as these are translated by the market into increases in the price of the firm's securities. However, it does not follow from this that the value of a stock is largely independent of a company's earnings and rests exclusively on the share of earnings which management chooses to pay out in dividends. It will be shown presently, following Modigliani and Miller that, perhaps paradoxically, it is the earnings potential and not the dividend policy of a firm which in some sense determines the "intrinsic value" of its securities.

It must also be emphasized that, as elsewhere in economic analysis, it is

closely the value of future earnings and share prices correspond in practice.

Security Pricing and the Use of Capital Resources

Moreover, it can be argued plausibly that the pricing of securities in accord with earnings prospects is precisely what is required for an efficient allocation of capital resources. For if the prices of the securities of an operating company did not correspond to its earnings, funds would not flow more readily to the firms best able to utilize them, where such ability is necessarily measured by prospective returns to the firm. An issue of a given number of securities by a firm with particularly promising investment opportunities need not, in such circumstances, yield a correspondingly large amount of money capital. Real resources would, as a consequence, be allocated imperfectly. Moreover, if security prices were divorced from earnings potential, the stock market could not be expected to serve as an effective disciplinary force capable of pressing management to maintain the efficiency of company operations. If a low earnings firm were as likely to encounter favorable funds market conditions as was one offering higher returns, a tangible incentive to efficiency would be destroyed. Thus the price of a security on the market is of critical importance for resource allocation, and we have good grounds for concern with the subject.

If the security market did have a structure which tended to produce prices corresponding to *long-run* competitive equilibrium we would have some presumption that all would automatically be well. All the usual conditions of long-run competitive equilibrium, the marginal equalities which guarantee (given the appropriate assumptions) that everything is optimal would apply equally here.

In such circumstances the price of the stock would, to begin with, reflect the marginal valuation of the security by its purchaser. Here

earnings potential *at the margin* which plays a critical role in what follows. But marginal earnings yields will vary with the scale of a firm's operations, as it takes advantage of a larger proportion of the investment opportunities which are available to it. Thus, as Lerner and Carleton have pointed out effectively, the theory of the valuation of securities must ultimately be integrated with an analysis of the firm's real investment (capital budgeting) calculations. See Lerner, Eugene M. and Willard T. Carleton, "The Integration of Capital Budgeting and Stock Valuation," *American Economic Review*, 54 (September 1964).

we encounter a complication—the utility obtained by holding a security is in some sense a derived demand—that is, the security is itself an instrument whose value stems from the stream of income it provides to its holder. But it is precisely this feature of the long-run competitive securities price which would guarantee that it did reflect the earnings prospects of the company. For in the long run the purchaser would be willing to pay only an amount equal to the yield which that security promises to offer him at the margin. By design this statement is left somewhat vague for, as already indicated, it will be more convenient to go into the relationship between company and stockholder earnings somewhat later in this chapter.

In addition to the demand adjustments implied in a long-run competitive equilibrium, it also must satisfy the usual supply condition which requires that the value of the security equal its marginal cost. Unfortunately, in the case of a stock, what we mean by its marginal cost is not even clear in principle. A great deal of controversy has centered about just this matter. We shall also see presently that whatever one decides to denote by the term, there is good reason to doubt that the market's valuation mechanism will serve to produce equality between a security's marginal cost and its price. Here we will find one of the major shortcomings of the securities market in practice, as compared with the usual theoretical allocation model.

Two Conflicting Views of Securities Pricing

It has already been suggested in this chapter that discussions of the determination of security prices can for our purposes be characterized in terms of two limiting cases. One of these two extreme types of explanation accounts for the price of a stock in terms of the value of the company whose securities are in question. In this type of analysis stock prices tend generally to be set systematically and rationally by a process which leads them to approximate the economic value of the real resources which they represent. However, the stock-pricing process is sometimes regarded in a totally different way. I am not suggesting that there are two opposing schools of thought between which there is a sharp and well-defined conflict. On the contrary, depending on the context, some writers appear at one point to consider the one model, sometimes the other (and more often, some in-between construct) as the more appropriate explanation of a particular phenomenon. Yet there is a very clear-cut distinction between the two extreme analytic frameworks and the distinction is important for our investigation.

This second limiting approach envisions the determination of stock prices, essentially, as a speculative and anticipatory phenomenon in which stock prices are what they are only because of what purchasers and sellers expect them to be. Thus, market values would largely or exclusively reflect the psychological state of security purchasers and sellers. In one extreme variant of this sort of model the earnings prospects of the firm only enter the pricing process because they constitute one among the many stimuli which happen to influence speculative anticipations as to what other speculators are going to do. This position has been most elegantly summarized by Keynes in a very well-known passage

... professional investment may be likened to those newspaper competitions in which the competitors have to pick out the six prettiest faces from a hundred photographs, the prize being awarded to the competitor whose choice most nearly corresponds to the average preferences of the competitors as a whole; so that each competitor has to pick, not those faces which he himself finds prettiest, but those which he thinks likeliest to catch the fancy of the other competitors, all of whom are looking at the problem from the same point of view. It is not a case of choosing those which, to the best of one's judgment, are really the prettiest, nor even those which average opinion genuinely thinks the prettiest. We have reached the third degree where we devote our intelligences to anticipating what average opinion expects the average opinion to be. And there are some, I believe, who practice the fourth, fifth and higher degrees.[2]

Superficial observation readily lends support to either of the views on the determination of stock prices which we are discussing. When there is an announcement of a piece of news about a company's earning prospects which disappoints current expectations, the price of its security can be expected to fall; so that security prices are quite sensitive to changes in the anticipated future returns of the firm. On

[2] John Maynard Keynes, *The General Theory of Employment, Interest and Money* (New York: Harcourt, Brace 1936), p. 156. Reprinted by permission of the publishers.

the other hand, many stock price movements seem to have no interpretation other than the one offered by Keynes unless one is prepared
to attribute absolute and total irrationality to security traders. A
sharp response to apparently irrelevant stimuli is a noteworthy feature
of stock price movements—an illustration frequently offered is the
response to the assassination of President Kennedy. Perhaps more to
the point was the response several years ago to the announcement by
one of the nation's largest firms that it had developed a process for the
production of artificial diamonds, whereupon there was an immediate
rise in the value of its outstanding securities that seems to have ex-
ceeded by far any plausible offhand evaluation of the potential
production of these stones.

The Random-Walk Hypothesis

As a matter of fact there is a growing accumulation of empirical
evidence suggesting that price behavior on the securities exchanges is
largely random. A number of highly competent investigators[3] have
with a remarkable degree of agreement concluded that the time-path
of stock market prices can be described in terms of what is called a
"random walk." By this we mean that the model which provides the
"best" description of the time-path of the price of any particular stock
predicts that in any future period that price will be equal to the price
of that same security in the immediately preceding period plus some
number randomly chosen. In other words, if we utilize only past price
data for that security and statistical methods no more powerful than
those employed by the authors,[4] any resulting deterministic prediction will, on the average, do no better than a random forecast. This
observation does not preclude the possibility that some statistical
data other than past stock prices can provide the basis for a

[3] Many of their reports and of the articles cited subsequently are reproduced
in Paul H. Cootner, ed., *The Random Character of Stock Market Prices* (Cambridge, Mass.: M. I. T. Press, 1964). There have, however, been a few questioning
comments. Thus see the discussion by Cootner (esp. pp. 194–5) and Alexander
(pp. 199–218) in the volume just cited.

[4] This reservation is necessary because it is always possible that there is some
comparatively subtle deterministic relationship which has managed to elude the
techniques employed by those who have studied the random-walk hypothesis.

satisfactory price forecast—past earnings might, for example, serve as a predictor of future security prices. But this would suggest that the historical behavior of earnings also constitute a random walk—for it is plausible that nonrandom independent variables will usually (though not necessarily) produce in their dependent variable behavior which is not perfectly random.

This remarkable result,[5] with its implications about the confidence one can have in stock market forecasting "systems" has been extended, and to a considerable extent, confirmed in a very sophisticated study conducted by Granger and Morgenstern.[6] These authors employ the relatively new methods of spectral analysis which permit the investigation of relationships corresponding to a wide range of time periods—as wide a range as is considered appropriate—to see whether any statistical patterns of significance can be determined. That is, spectral methods permit us to test whether randomness only characterizes the relationship between stock prices at date t and those of the preceding few days, or whether it also applies to longer periods. The Morgenstern-Granger study, for all practical purposes, agrees with the earlier random-walk conclusions. It shows that, except possibly for very long movements—cycles or trends whose duration is a decade or longer—randomness is indeed the order of the day in the behavior of individual security prices. One concludes, then, that forecasting over the period of time for which most stocks are normally held is at best an extremely hazardous and at worst a totally hopeless business. True, secular inflation and other related pressures have carried the market upward over the long run so that rather good returns have typically been yielded to a representative

---

[5] It should be emphasized that the result is remarkable because it is so difficult to find a set of really random numbers. For example, the calculation of tables of random numbers requires extremely subtle methods and even these have been known to fail; that is, subsequent tests have revealed significant departures from randomness in some such tables. Thus, while it may not be surprising that a time-series of stock prices would in some sense exhibit "erratic" patterns, it might appear much less likely in advance, that no significant departures from randomness could be discerned in such a series. Perhaps, though, this is only a reflection on the power of our statistical tools.

[6] C. W. J. Granger and O. Morgenstern, "Spectral Analysis of New York Stock Market Prices," *Kyklos*, 16 (1963).

security purchaser.[7] But, apparently, statistical analysis of past price data cannot be relied upon to produce returns better than the stock market average.[8]

The evidence of randomness in the behavior of security prices may increase our doubts about the standard picture of the underlying pricing mechanism of the stock market. If stock market prices were to behave in accord with the dictates of a simple valuation mechanism, one might suspect that their history would be dominated far less completely by randomness than these studies have indicated to be the case. True, the prosperity of the firms whose securities are sold on the market may fluctuate somewhat erratically. There would then be little conflict between the random behavior of stock prices and the implications of an equilibrium stock-pricing model. But since what is pertinent in such a model is not the day-by-day earnings of the firms but their long-range prospects, one may well be skeptical about

---

[7] L. Fisher and J. H. Lorie, "Rates of Return on Investments in Common Stocks," *The Journal of Business*, 37 (January 1964).

[8] A second line of statistical investigation may also be relevant here. With remarkable persistence, Dr. Benoit Mandelbrot has examined the application to economic phenomena of a type of probability distribution whose most interesting characteristic for our present discussion is that it has an infinite variance or standard deviation. It may be recalled rather briefly that the variance is a measure of dispersion of a statistic. If the standard deviation is large it means that the average value of the statistics in question is not terribly representative because at least a few of the numbers differ from the average by a very considerable amount. Thus the standard deviation can be very helpful in forecasting. In effect, it provides confidence limits telling us how widely observed results are likely to differ from their predicted values. But Mandelbrot and, after him, Fama, have maintained on the basis of their statistical investigations that as more and more observations of stock market prices are collected, the calculated standard deviation of these figures will grow without limit. See Benoit Mandelbrot, "The Variation of Certain Speculative Prices," *The Journal of Business*, 36 (October 1963) and Eugene F. Fama, "Mandelbrot and the Stable Paretian Hypothesis," *The Journal of Business*, same issue. However, Godfrey, Granger and Morgenstern report that in the data which they examined " . . . there is no evidence of the long tails [in the histogram of first differences of prices] which Mandelbrot's hypothesis would predict. . . . No evidence was found in any of [the] series that the process by which they were generated behaved as if it possessed an infinite variance." (M. D. Godfrey, C. W. J. Granger and O. Morgenstern, "The Random-Walk Hypothesis of Stock Market Behavior," *Kyklos*, 17 (1964).

the suggestion that the value of the corporation really behaves in the manner of a random walk.

Yet even here one can easily argue the other way—one can suggest that a stock's price is determined not by the company's long-term earnings prospects, but by the public's *expectations* about these earnings. And random fluctuations in the quarterly earnings reports can easily lead investors to revise drastically their long-term anticipations (the relatively elastic-expectations case) thereby imparting randomness to stock price behavior. While this explanation seems to have merit, unfortunately, it will not do here—it will not lend effective support to the view that the market will price securities in accord with a deterministic mechanism and that it will select prices which approximate those that will produce an optimal allocation of resources. Two comments should make this clear.

1. If very temporary variations in reported company-earnings can of themselves panic many members of the public into a sharp revision in expectations, even though long-term prospects are not nearly so volatile, the resulting market prices must frequently depart by a considerable margin from the level which is called for on grounds of resource allocation—a departure which need not be confined to the short run.

2. If investor's valuation of company stocks were affected only periodically by occasional pieces of information such as quarterly earnings reports, then stock prices should not behave randomly over the very short periods, i.e., for the period between the receipt of two such data. Yet, the evidence for the random-walk hypothesis is apparently just as strong in the very short period case as it is for longer periods.

There is also a rather more subtle theoretical analysis which attempts to account for the random behavior of security prices and which carries with it the implication that randomness is the product of investor rationality and is exactly what one must expect of the dynamics of the equilibrating process. Since the analysis is illuminating in itself, and somewhat relevant to our central topic, I shall digress briefly to discuss it.

The Dynamics of Informed Investment

Godfrey, Granger and Morgenstern discuss the effects on a competitive stock market of the receipt of information which permits effective prediction of future prices. They point out that the reactions of buyers and sellers can be expected to cause changes in present and prospective prices that eliminate completely any advantage which the information confers. For example, suppose it is judged by the body of security traders that the price of security x can safely be expected to rise by ten percent above what had formerly been anticipated. The current price of the stock will be bid up at once and by an amount such that nothing is left to be gained by the purchase of this stock except what it would have yielded in the absence of the piece of information in question. That is, the market's action may be expected to raise current price by ten percent also. For unless price has risen by this amount it will pay investors who possess the pertinent information to increase their demand from its initial level, and thus current price will be driven higher. But once the current price has been adjusted fully, no further profit can accrue from knowledge of the fact which led to the price change; the investor will be no better off than he had been in his previous state of ignorance.

Godfrey, Granger and Morgenstern conclude that the only price changes which need not be eliminated by the process are those which are unforeseen. But if investors are rational *and can calculate perfectly* the *only* unpredictable changes are those which are random. Thus the very equilibration process will serve to eliminate anything but random movements on the stock exchange (and possibly on any other form of well-organized market, for that matter). Hence, it is suggested, the statistical evidence which supports the random-walk hypothesis may even lend credence to the view that pricing on the stock exchange is an extremely efficient exercise in the employment of rational calculation.

There is no question that the preceding discussion sheds a great deal of light on the working of the market and represents a very real contribution. Yet our suspicions should be aroused because the observed degree of randomness confirms the applicability of the proposed pricing model just a bit *too* well. I have occasionally suggested than in an economist's statistical calculations an outcome far more disturbing than a very low correlation is one that is surprisingly high. And here we have an analogous reason to be disquieted—we have a model which under ideal conditions would eliminate everything but random behavior, and the behavior of the market seems to conform exactly with that prediction.

As a matter of fact, there are specific reasons why one would *not* have expected so close a relationship; why in a real world operating in accord with our model, though random changes might well constitute the preponderant portion of price movement, there would remain at least some observable residue of systematic behavior.

First of all, for the equilibrating process to eliminate all systematic price movements which can be traced by the econometrician, the stock market trader's ability to discover such systematic components would have to be every bit as good as the statistician's. Relationships which can only be revealed by powerful statistical tools could not have been acted upon "perfectly" and thereby eliminated *completely* by investors who are privy to no special information, and whose acquaintance with econometric methods is limited. Of course, experience may well teach the professional investor to do a very creditable job of it just as we may expect (following Professor Machlup) that the businessman's instinct and observation can enable him roughly to approximate marginal decision calculations. But such adjustments will be imperfect at best and one would think that careful analysis of the data would reveal this imperfection. Surely, then, the observation that investor behavior has left the field *exclusively* to random price movements requires some additional explanation.

There are yet other considerations of greater theoretical import which lead us to this conclusion. In a real dynamic process one would not expect information to be diffused through the market, or to be acted upon instantaneously. Rather, knowledge would be diffused slowly and imperfectly like an innovation in the Schumpeterian process. Time is apt to be required for those who discover information to reap their rewards, and only gradually[9] as it spreads to other traders will their profit opportunities be eliminated.

---

[9] Of course, on the securities markets adjustments can occur much more quickly than in a physical production process. Where the manufacturer of a new product may need several years of differential advantage to recoup his investment, the possessor of information pertinent to the stock market can harvest his gains far more quickly. It should be recognized that only a small fraction of

True, in principle even one trader can take advantage of "inside" information to an extent sufficient to eliminate the profit opportunities which it provides. But to do so he might require extremely great capital resources. He must also consider the implications of his piece of information for future stock prices to be very near certain, for otherwise the increasing risk which accompanies the commitment of a larger and larger proportion of his wealth to the opportunity under discussion would finally cause him to bring his involvement to a halt. In other words, his finite supply of funds, and the presence of risk will normally impose on any one trader an equilibrium (maximal) figure limiting the amount he is willing to speculate on the opportunity brought to light by his inside information. That being the case, we can expect the influence of information to manifest itself slowly so that only after some discernable period would it permit the elimination of the corresponding systematic time-pattern in the price of the security. As has already been stated, the entire sequence of events must then constitute a Schumpeterian process, something which should hardly surprise us when we recall that Schumpeter explicitly included the utilization of previously unexploited knowledge in his list of innovations.

All of this discussion has, I trust, offered us some insight into the equilibrating process which accomplishes the absorption of information by a well designed competitive market. It seems to be a very good arrangement, with even the frictions in its mechanism playing a most useful role. For it is the delays in its operations which permit rewards to be reaped by those who improve the state of knowledge, and which therefore leads to the expenditure of effort on the gathering of information. Yet these very imperfections would permit some non-random price movements on an exchange operated on the

the existing amount of some security need be moved in order to produce an adjustment in its price. Thus, a small number of informed professional traders can do a creditable job of producing fairly rapid equilibrating price movements.

However, in the stock market there is a very important element working in the other direction. Because of the high degree of uncertainty involved, investors will normally disagree in their anticipations. For otherwise very little trading would occur. Frequently, then, a given piece of information may be interpreted differently by different traders and the dynamics of the adjustment of opinions to one another can increase the amount of time required by the adjustment process.

TRUE VALUE WILL OUT

principles described.[10] If in fact *only* random price behavior can be discerned in stock price statistics, one is tempted to surmise that the operation of the exchange differs in some important respect from this ideal competitive adjustment model.[11]

[10] I have, however, come across evidence of surprisingly good approximation to perfection in another speculative market—the race track. A study of the odds calculated on the tote boards at several tracks suggests that—presumably through the agency of the bets made by the professionals—all opportunities for profit by systematic bettings patterns are eliminated. Bets at ten to one will in the long run come off almost exactly as badly as bets at three to one. See Harold Schiffman, Donald E. Mintz and Samuel Messick, "Successive Intervals Scaling of Money at the Race Track" (Princeton: Educational Testing Service, June 1963) (mimeographed).

[11] For a variety of reasons it must be admitted that my discussion of the random walk materials may well overstate their implications for our purposes. For example, it has been suggested to me that there is no necessary inconsistency between a standard analytic model of price determination and a time series of prices which constitutes a random walk. That is, it is felt that fortuitous events on the markets characteristically produce patterns of shifts in the pertinent graphs which could easily lead to random price behavior.

This is easily illustrated. The simplest of supply-demand econometric models includes only the two (endogenous) variables, price (P_t) and quantity (Q_t). Thus we have

$$P_t = a - bQ_t + U \quad \text{(demand equation)}$$
$$Q_t = c + kP_t + V \quad \text{(supply equation)}$$

where a, b, c and k are constants, and U and V are random disturbance variables representing fortuitous influences on the operations of the market. (The specialist will readily note that these equations are of the troublesome variety called "unidentified" by the econometricians.) Now, substituting from the second equation into the first we obtain $P_t = a - bc - bkP_t - bV + U$ so that

$$P_t = \frac{a-bc}{1+bk} + \frac{U-bv}{1+bk} \quad \text{i.e., } P_t = \alpha + W$$

where α is a constant and W is the random variable $\dfrac{U-bV}{1+bK}$. This is clearly the expression for a variable whose time path is a random walk.

However, it is easy to see that results might be quite different if exogenous variables were involved in the model. For example, if demand were also affected by the level of income, Y, our demand equation would become $P_t = \alpha - bQ + rY$, and our final price expression would then be

$$P_t = \alpha + \beta Y + W,$$

which need not constitute random-walk relationship unless Y is itself a random variable.

Stock Prices Under Long-Run Competitive Equilibrium

There are various reasons, then, for suspecting that security pricing does not follow as well structured and systematic a pattern as might have been expected from competitive pricing theory. Let us therefore examine the structure of the market a little more closely to see which of its features help to account for this apparent divergence. The most obvious place to look is the demand side, at the psychological peculiarities of the purchasers of stocks. And, as a matter of fact, oddities in the behavior of security prices are commonly attributed to the irrationality of many of those who trade in them. This is not meant to imply that I agree with such a view. Rather, I shall argue presently that even if stock purchasers and sellers acted as rationally as can reasonably be expected under the circumstances all the oddities that have been observed in stock market prices might very well continue to manifest themselves.

I have already emphasized that the offer to purchase a security is in essence a derived demand, the value of the security not being intrinsically determined in some sense, but depending on the future returns which it is expected to bring in. In this respect the valuation of a security is very similar to that of money. Unlike an ordinary consumer good, the benefit which one obtains by holding some currency is necessarily highly dependent on the level of its purchasing power. And the circumstances of a security are analogous. The utility of such a share is also inseparable from its current and prospective market values. Moreover, in this respect, security valuation is much more complex and elusive than that of money. Expectations do have some role to play in the latter—the demand for cash may be decreased when people come to expect an inflation which will erode its value and it may be raised when potential investors foresee an imminent opportunity to purchase assets on favorable terms. The demand for money must also be based on prognostication of prospective purchases. But such plans are, to a large extent, under the purchaser's control and may even be definite and explicit. In general, it seems reasonable to suppose that the magnitudes of the cash holdings of most individuals are determined by inertia and institutional considerations (such as the magnitude of the minimum cash balance required on a checking account) and that the value of cash to them is influenced only slightly by their expectations.

The value of a security, on the other hand, depends almost exclusively on one's view of the future. One consequence is that for all practical purposes it is almost impossible to disentangle stock purchases which are made for investment from those which are undertaken for speculative purposes. In either case a stock is obviously bought with an eye to the future and in the hope that future developments will prove favorable to the buyer.[12]

If, then, it is agreed that the utility of a security depends primarily on anticipations and if expectations are highly volatile, we arrive at an obvious explanation for unsystematic behavior in stock market prices. Add to this the very high degree of uncertainty which obscures future security prices—uncertainty which, as we have seen, may often make calculation of prospects next to impossible, and it is not difficult to understand the appearance of some degree of caprice and confusion in the behavior of security purchasers.

But the classical equilibrium mechanism is composed of more than just the demand side of the market which we have so far been discussing. In an ideal competitive market price movements generate supply responses which bring prices back into line with marginal costs in the long run. Prices which are high in comparison with costs produce an increased flow of offerings that drive prices downward and the reverse occurs if prices fall very low. This much we learned from the classical cost of production theory of value. That analysis tells us that prices cannot depart for very long or very far from marginal costs for, if they do, either exit or entry of firms will bring them back into line.

But on the stock exchange there are several extremely important reasons why such a sequence of events will not normally take place. At any given moment, the bulk of stocks traded is composed of

[12] There is another important analogue between the equilibrating mechanism in the money market and that in the market for securities. While any one trader can at any time increase or reduce his holdings of securities, the amount available to the body of traders as a whole can be considered relatively fixed. But while the body of traders has no direct control over the number of pieces of paper (stock certificates) which they hold, they do determine the market value of these securities through their influence on stock *prices*.

holdings of old securities rather than of new issues. For example, between 1959 and 1962 the total value of shares turned over per annum on the New York Stock Exchange ranged between 38 and 53 billion dollars; the market value of all stocks listed on the exchange varied between 307 and 388 billions, whereas the net sale of new issues *of all stocks* in the United States during these same years ranged from 0.6 to 2.6 billions.[13] Thus the latter clearly constituted an insignificant proportion of either of the former. On a market in which the bulk of the supply consists of ancient inventory, the influence of cost of production on price is likely to be weak. It is still true, even in such circumstances, that there must in the long run be equality between price and marginal cost. No matter how small the flow of new supplies, its magnitude will be regulated so as to produce the appropriate marginal equality when competitive equilibrium is achieved. But it is hardly legitimate to conclude from this that under such circumstances price is still effectively *determined* by marginal cost. Rather one can more reasonably argue that it is marginal cost which is controlled by market price. In such a market the supply will simply have to adapt itself to the market clearing price which is, largely, independently determined.[14]

There are a number of other markets in which inventory provides the bulk of the items traded. For example, the precious metals markets have this characteristic, and in communities where construction has been lagging because population is not growing, it is true of housing. Perhaps the most notable illustration is the market for painting and sculpture. And in each of these markets it is notorious

[13] Sources: New York Stock Exchange *Fact Book*, 1963 and *Federal Reserve Bulletin* (November 1964). Common and preferred stocks are both included in these figures but mutual funds shares are excluded. The figures are net of retirements.

[14] Precisely the same sort of difficulty has been called to our attention by Professor Viner in his discussion of the Keynesian view that the rate of interest is determined exclusively by liquidity preference. It is just as reasonable to argue, Viner has suggested in conversation, that the price of cigars is regulated by the utility function of female cigar smokers because, surely, at the margin the price must be equal to the marginal utility of cigars to any of their feminine consumers. See Jacob Viner, "Comments on My 1936 Review of Keynes' *General Theory*," in Robert Lekachman, ed., *Keynes' General Theory*; *Reports of Three Decades* (New York: St. Martins Press, 1964).

that the dependence of price on cost of production is often quite weak.

I have already alluded to a second peculiar difficulty which besets the equilibrating mechanism of the stock market. For suppliers to behave consistently in a manner which drives price toward marginal cost of production, it is necessary that they know the magnitudes of their costs, at least approximately. If a supplier has no way to calculate his marginal costs he will not know when price exceeds it, and so he cannot be expected to institute the appropriate equilibrating supply response. The cost of supplying a new security issue is an extremely slippery concept. There are, of course, some fairly obvious components—the cost of preparing the information required by the SEC, the various associated fees, etc. But perhaps the most significant component of the cost of a share of a new issue is its opportunity cost—the prospective income which a current security holder is forced to forego as a result of the purchase of this share by someone else. That is, of course, what is denoted by the standard term "the cost of capital." Unfortunately, it is not very easy to decide what this cost of capital *ought* to measure, much less to determine just how one might go about the calculation. The fact is that the entire matter is still far from settled and even the theorists disagree sharply on many pertinent issues. Thus, the cost of production of new securities is not defined unambiguously even in the theoretical literature, let alone in the decision procedures of the suppliers—the corporations which issue the stocks.[15]

There is a final and most important reason for the failure of suppliers to play the role which is expected of them in the long-run competitive equilibrating process. This reason resides in the nature of the market structure and the system of control which characterizes the suppliers of securities. The firms in question are clearly not pure competitors. The bulk of the companies whose securities are listed on the stock exchanges are oligopolistic in character, in which there is, frequently, some separation between ownership and management. As a result, their behavior is quite different from that of the competitive supplier. Indeed, their security supply patterns differ

---

[15] For a good selection of some of the standard writings on the cost of capital see Ezra Solomon, *The Management of Corporate Capital* (Glencoe, Illinois: The Free Press, 1959), Part III.

far more from what would be expected of a competitive firm than is the case with the products that they manufacture. Whereas an upward shift in the demand for a product of one of these firms is likely to call forth some increase in its supply, no such response in the supply of their securities can usually be expected. For a variety of reasons, some of which will be discussed in the last chapter of this book, those in control of the operations of the American corporation have, at least in recent years, not materially increased their supply of equity in their firms even when the market's terms—its exceedingly high price-earnings ratios—appeared to be particularly favorable. As a matter of fact, many corporate managements have in recent years tried very hard to avoid supplying any new equity at all.

We see, then, that on the stock market several critical components of the long-run competitive pricing mechanism do not function in the traditional manner. Prices have effectively been insulated from each of the forces which one expects to hold them near competitive equilibrium values—from the tangible and relatively stationary use value toward which demand behavior can drive market price, and from the cost of production which regulates price through the responsiveness of the suppliers.

Theory of Strategy and the Pricing of Securities

What, then, is the outcome of this discussion? It would appear to suggest that the Keynesian view of the pricing of securities is ultimately right. There would seem to be little support for the contention that the market values of securities are determined systematically by their costs and their prospective yields. Rather the pricing process must, it would seem, be viewed as the net outcome of the confrontation of individual traders' fortuitous hunches and perhaps little else. Yet there is more to be said about the matter. One can look more carefully into the interaction process which determines the valuations of the traders who, like Keynes' newspaper photo contestants, are in the business of trying to guess what will be done by other participants whose motivations are similar to their own. But to analyze such a process one must turn from ordinary equilibrium theory to the analysis of problems of strategy—to game theory and some of its related developments.

How might a rational security trader act in the circumstances postulated? Surely he will not simply throw up his hands and delegate his decisions to a random device. Rather, one would expect him to hunt about for signals which offer him clues about the prospective behavior of his fellow traders, utilizing his knowledge that they, too, will be searching for the same sort of information.

There is a great deal to be learned here from Schelling's analysis of what he has called "focal points."[16] Schelling has devised a series of games in which people are asked to coordinate their activities on the basis of very little information. For example, he has proposed the following among a series of problems:

> You are to meet somebody in New York City. You have not been instructed where to meet; you have no prior understanding with the person on where to meet; and you cannot communicate with each other. You are simply told that you will have to guess where to meet and that he is being told the same thing and that you will just have to try to make your guesses coincide (p. 56).

A sample of persons asked this question in New Haven, Connecticut (Professor Schelling was then at Yale) showed an absolute majority managing to get together at Grand Central Station at the information booth, and virtually all of them succeeded in meeting at twelve noon. Schelling concluded

> These problems are artificial, but they illustrate the point. People *can* often concert their intentions or expectations with others if each knows that the other is trying to do the same. Most situations—perhaps every situation for people who are practiced at this kind of game—provide some clue for coordinating behavior, some focal point for each person's expectation of what the other expects him to expect to be expected to do. Finding the key, or rather finding *a* key . . . may depend on imagination more than on logic; it may depend on analogy, precedent, accidental arrangement, symmetry, aesthetic or geometric configuration, casuistic reasoning, and who the parties are and what they know about each other. . . . It is not being asserted that they will always find an obvious answer to the question; but the chances of their doing so are ever so much greater than the bare logic of abstract random probabilities would ever suggest.

[16] Thomas C. Schelling, *The Strategy of Conflict* (Cambridge, Mass.: Harvard Univ. Press, 1960), esp. pp. 54 ff. Reprinted by permission of the publishers.

A prime characteristic of most of these 'solutions' to the problems, that is, of the clues or coordinators or focal points, is some kind of prominence or conspicuousness (p. 57).

Much of the behavior that is observed on the stock market can easily be accounted for in these terms. Response to apparent irrelevancies such as presidential illness, instead of appearing a manifestation of panic or caprice is seen as a rational response to a conspicuous signal which is seized upon by people searching desperately for information.

This hypothesis can also account for whatever degree of concurrence between security prices and company earnings prospects one can observe in the market. For news that affects the future prosperity of the firm is surely a focal point *par excellence* about which the traders (each hoping that he has observed the signal a bit early) can rally in their attempt to anticipate one another's behavior. On this view, prospective earnings serve in the pricing process not as the instrument of competitive pressure which one would expect from long-run equilibrium theory but as a means for coordinating expectations. I am, I must confess, attracted to this Schelling-Keynes model of market behavior as a plausible explanation of the facts, though it offers no very promising basis for the erection of a deterministic theory which is also aesthetically satisfying.

Yet there is at least one more thing to be said in support of a theory of stock prices which is closer to the received equilibrium model. For this purpose we must turn to some of the recent contributions of Professors Modigliani and Miller.

Dividend Payments and the Valuation of Shares

Let us inquire somewhat more closely into the relationship between the value of a firm's share and its prospective earnings in a model utilizing rather strong rationality assumptions. In the process there will emerge an extremely persuasive defense of the orthodox view of their relationship—the position that the value of a share is dependent ultimately on company earnings. We will then have come full circle and end up with an ingenious defense of the proposition upon which, up to this point, we have been casting doubt, the view that the stock market tends to set prices in the manner appropriate for an efficient allocation of capital resources.

To get at the relationship between stock prices and earnings we will have to proceed somewhat by indirection. Our discussion will first show why in a rational world without uncertainty stock prices will not be affected by the strategic considerations which determine a company's rate of dividend payout. It will then turn out that in this model prices do follow long-run earnings rather than dividend payout rates.

We begin, then, with Professors Miller and Modigliani's illuminating proposition that in a perfect market, where perfect certainty and rationality prevail, and where there are neither taxes nor transaction costs, the dividend policy of a corporation is economically irrelevant —it will "affect neither the current price of its shares nor the total return to its shareholders."[17]

The logic of the Miller-Modigliani position can be summarized very briefly in the following rather oversimplified form. We shall proceed by means of an analogue of a controlled experiment, in which the rate of dividend payout is varied, and examine its effects *when all other things are held constant*. Thus, we suppose a company is considering a D dollar total current dividend payment to be divided among its stockholders, and that every shareholder and potential shareholder knows (and knows that others know) that the company will replace the money by means of a new equity issue, but that this decision will have no other effect on future company plans (including planned future investments, earnings and dividend payments). Because there will be no real change in the future operations of the company, the *total* value of all of the firms' shares outstanding at the end of the period, $V(t+1)$, must also remain unchanged. But since the company has not revised its investment plans, it must replace the D dollars it has just paid out by issuing D dollars in new shares. In that case the value of the shares held by the original stockholders at the end of the period must be $V(t+1)-D$, that is, it must equal the total value of the firm's stocks minus the value of the stocks that will belong to others.

[17] Merton H. Miller and Franco Modigliani, "Dividend Policy, Growth and the Valuation of Shares," *Journal of Business*, 34 (October 1961), 412–15.

In summary, the current stockholders' present equity is worth the D dollar dividend payment plus the V(t+1)−D dollar value of its claim on the company's future, a net value of V(t−1) which is totally unaffected by the magnitude of the current dividend payment, be it zero or something well in excess of the company's earnings.[18] We conclude that, *given the firm's planned investments and future earnings and dividend payments*, it should make no difference to the shareholder whether he receives any dividends or, instead, the company retains these earnings to finance its investments.[19,20]

Miller and Modigliani go on to maintain that their proposition can be extended to situations that encompass a variety of imperfections, provided that investors satisfy a postulate which they label "symmetric market rationality." This assumption means that every participant in the market for shares is an efficient wealth maximizer who is indifferent between the receipt of dividends or their equivalent in capital gains, and that he believes the same thing to be true of all

[18] For simplicity this very brief summary has ignored the discounting problems involved in comparing dividend payments at the beginning of the period with the value of the firm at its end. We can avoid this problem by assuming the entire process to take place instantaneously. Miller and Modigliani are, of course, much more careful on this point and their mathematical expressions are, as a result, somewhat more complicated.

[19] The popular practice of stock dividends payment (that is, the issue of additional shares to current stockholders) can be considered as a kind of mnemonic device to remind the stockholder that the current cash dividends that he forgoes are, in essence, simply additional equity investments undertaken for him. These will ultimately be reflected in the total investment value of the shares. Of course, the economic significance of stock dividends in this respect is nil. But we now see that in the circumstances posited the distinction between cash and stock dividends is also irrelevant!

It should be pointed out, lest the preceding comment be misunderstood, that stock dividends are not necessarily a manifestation of irrationality either on the part of management or shareholders. For example, a stock dividend may serve as a means of communication whereby management, *without committing itself*, indicates to the market that company earnings prospects are favorable.

[20] We have so far only considered the current-period decision on dividend payments. However, as Miller and Modigliani have pointed out, since the period that we have chosen to call the "current period" is perfectly arbitrary, it follows that dividend policy at any and hence every particular future date is equally irrelevant!

other participants in the market. From this they deduce that each
investor should expect dividends to be irrelevant to all other investors and that therefore dividends should be irrelevant to his own
security trading decisions.

In an earlier note[21] I argued that in some circumstances there is
reason to question the plausibility of their basic assumption. As
the authors point out, " . . . if an ordinarily rational investor had good
reason to believe that other investors would not behave rationally,
then it might well be rational for him to adopt a strategy he would
otherwise have rejected as irrational" (p. 428).

Once such defensive "irrationality" is recognized as a possibility,
no investor can be expected to have confidence that others will refrain
from it. We find ourselves in the classic game-theoretic situation of
the prisoners' dilemma, where two separately interrogated culprits
could both gain if they simultaneously refused to confess, but, because
each lacks perfect confidence in the other, he is likely, on rational
grounds, to find the temptation to "sing" quite irresistible. The
individual investor, knowing that all can gain by the simultaneous
exercise of rationality will no more be moved by this consideration
than will the small farmer who knows that if he and every other
farmer independently cuts his output by fifty percent, all of them will
gain. Each, on rational grounds, will be motivated to behave in an
"irrational" manner because he knows that others will, for the same
reason, have rational grounds to do so as well.

It is plausible that current dividend rates will produce this type of
response, especially since (as Miller and Modigliani pointed out and
document) it seems to be a standard view that the shares of low
payout companies will sell at a discount (p. 432, esp. n. 33). To the
extent that this is the general expectation of security purchasers, even
though they consider it a manifestation of irrationality, they will have
no option but to behave in a manner that makes the prediction come
true. We would then expect that perfectly rational investors would
have no choice but to place a subjective valuation lower than they

[21] W. J. Baumol, "On Dividend Policy and Market Imperfection," *The Journal
of Business*, 36 (January 1963). Much of this section is adapted from that note.
Also, see the reply by Miller and Modigliani in the same issue. Reprinted by
permission of the publishers.

would have otherwise on the companies that retain a relatively large percentage of their earnings, and that this reasoning would provide its own justification—the stocks of these companies would sell at a discount as compared with issues paying more generous dividends.[22]

In my original discussion I had also suggested that there was really nothing the individual security purchaser could or should do about such undervaluation in terms of his own interest. The fact that a share is "undervalued" according to the Miller-Modigliani criterion does not, I believed, imply that low payout stocks are a bargain to be grabbed up by the rational investor. For if they were undervalued when purchased and undervalued when sold, they would offer no extraordinary gain to their purchaser. In correspondence and in their reply, Miller and Modigliani showed that this assertion was correct only in the very special case of shares which pay no dividends at all.

Though they gave it no emphasis, they produced a most important theorem which brings us back to the central issue of this chapter. This is what I would like to call the "true value will out" theorem. That paradoxical proposition shows that in the long run, even if a stock offers a relatively low payout rate and is consistently undervalued by the market, it will yield a full measure of returns to the holder of the security. That is, if two shares represent rights over equal potential earnings per dollar of investment, but one share offers its holders a lower dividend rate than the other with the remainder being plowed back into the firm, in the long run both shares will approach the same stream of dividends in terms of capitalized present value! The present value of the low payout dividend stream will asymptotically approach the present value of the stream provided by the other security as the evaluation horizon grows infinitely large. This means that the owner of an undervalued share will have bought an equally valuable stream of dividends at a lower cost to himself. It

---

[22] Here, then, we have returned to the prisoners' dilemma argument. Each investor is forced to behave irrationally because he fears other investors will have fears similar to his own. The argument is somewhat weaker than in the case of the farm problem analogy employed above because each farmer would find it profitable to expand his supply even if he were fully confident that other farmers would not do so. The prisoner and the investor, alike, are forced into defensive irrationality only because they suspect others will also be forced into it.

follows therefore, that any investor is a fool, or acts on bad information, if he does not seek out such undervalued securities in preference
to higher dividend paying stocks. It can even be shown that the buyer
of the undervalued shares need not wait indefinitely for his greater
rewards per dollar of funds laid out. At the end of the first dividend-
payment period he will already come out ahead of the purchaser of
comparable high payout securities and his accumulated differential
gains will increase with the passage of every additional dividend
period. This will be so even if he chooses at some intermediate
stage to resell his stock and finds that the market is still undervaluing
it at the same rate, that is, at the same percentage discount as when
he had purchased it originally. Thus it would appear that earnings do
ultimately and solely determine the value to be derived by share-
holding and that if shareholders do learn at all well from their
experience, their purchasing patterns will, in the long run, force stock
prices to conform rather closely to these prospective earnings opportunities of the firms whose shares they buy.

It is not very difficult to supply a rigorous proof of our theorem and
one is offered in the appendix to this chapter. An intuitive explanation is only a little harder to provide. Basically, the logic of the
argument is that the firm which offers lower dividends, that is, a
lower proportion of dividends to earnings, will reinvest more and,
therefore, its absolute earnings will grow faster. Thus, even with a
fixed relatively low dividend-payout rate, rapidly growing earnings
will, in the long run, provide sufficiently increased dividend payments
to make up for the dividends which were denied the shareholder
earlier. In fact, in the limit, the reinvestment will provide exactly the
right rate of growth of earnings and hence, of dividend payments, to
make up (with interest) for the dividends which were lost through the
lower dividend-payout ratio. Thus undervaluation of such a security
offers stock purchasers a cheap claim on future dividend growth. Only
if dividends are actually zero so that the company retains all of its
earnings is this form of benefit denied to the purchaser of an undervalued security.[23]

[23] Professor Malkiel has pointed out to me that things are still not all gravy for
the shareholder in the undervalued firm. If that company decides to enter into the
capital market and obtain more funds by the issue of new shares, the under-

We conclude from all this that virtuous management brings its own rewards; that efficiency in operations and attractive future earnings prospects must apparently provide correspondingly attractive returns to investors so that no matter what the company's dividend policies, rationality will force investors to act in such a way that prices will be governed by the earnings ability of the companies.

Where Do We Stand?

We end up in a mildly uncomfortable position. We have arrived at a series of strong and apparently well-grounded results which, unfortunately, seem to conflict with one another. There are good a priori reasons to expect stock prices to depend on the earnings prospects of the firm, but there are also persuasive arguments which maintain that whatever correspondence there is in fact is accounted for only by the vagaries of investor strategy. Yet for our present purposes matters are not all that unsettled. We can, I think, say that we have arrived at two rather important conclusions:

1. While, as was suggested in the preceding chapter, the market may yield tolerable approximations to short-run competitive equilibrium, the long-run competitive mechanism, as ordinarily conceived, functions on the stock exchange only very imperfectly if at all. This is so because large and critical components of that machinery either are not there or just do not function. The overwhelming difficulties which effectively preclude comprehensive and reliable forecasting constitute only the most important reason why the demand side of the market cannot be expected to supply the knowledgeable utility-calculating individuals who populate our abstract models. The behavior of the supply side is at least as far removed from that which is traditionally assigned to this sector. The very concept "marginal cost of security supply" is under a cloud, and offerings of new stock seem almost totally unresponsive to price changes.

valuation of that company's stock will place it at a disadvantage as compared to other firms. This is, of course, true, but it should be recognized that our low dividend-payout firm will already be getting a relatively large amount of money for investment purposes by the very nature of its mode of operation—its high plowback rate. Only if management issues new shares frequently and in relatively large amounts will the initial purchaser of that company's stock lose the differential advantage offered to him by the undervaluation of the securities he purchased.

2. Yet we have strong reason to suspect that in a rough and ready way, security prices do follow closely the developments in company prospects. Whether they do so as a consequence of rationality of the Modigliani-Miller variety, or good strategic considerations of the sort suggested by Schelling, the result is likely to be somewhat similar. What remains to be investigated is how closely the market follows the appropriate information about the company, whether it is seriously misled by temporary aberrations in earnings patterns, whether it misguidedly places heavy weight on dividend policy, etc. The implications of this for our evaluation of the efficiency of the securities market as an allocator of capital are somewhat ambiguous. They do suggest that in the markets pricing will often not be too far from the mark but that this will not be the result of the workings of the normal regulators of the competitive mechanism, a mechanism that simply cannot be relied upon to yield the prices required for an optimal allocation of capital resources.

The economist's concluding plea for empirical research has come to partake of the character of the local politician's ringing defense of motherhood. Yet, I must agree with Miller and Modigliani that the questions which have been raised in this chapter are largely matters requiring empirical materials to be used as a basis for their analysis— they cannot be settled by a priori reasoning alone. Unfortunately, there are all sorts of booby traps which beset empirical study of the process whereby the market values securities and the determination of the variables which are of greatest importance in this process.[24] Happily, a variety of such investigations are now under way, many of them directed by outstanding members of our profession. There remains plenty of room for others to join them.

[24] A number of these have been pointed out by Modigliani and M. H. Miller. Modigliani and M. H. Miller, "The Cost of Capital, Corporation Finance and the Theory of Investment," *American Economic Review*, 48 (June 1958), pp. 281–8, and "Reply," same journal, 49 (September 1959), pp. 666–8. See also Irwin Friend and Marshall Puckett, "Dividends and Stock Prices," same journal, 54 (September 1964).

APPENDIX TO CHAPTER THREE

SOME THEOREMS ON UNDERVALUATION OF LOW DIVIDEND STOCKS

Some Propositions on Undervalued Stocks

It is frequently asserted that investor rationality should make the price earnings ratio of a stock an increasing function of the company's dividend payout rate. In other words, it is suggested that the market may price at a relative discount the stocks of a company which has a policy of paying a small proportion of its earnings out in dividends.[25]

For example, suppose companies *A* and *B* have equal earnings prospects for both current and anticipated investment and are equally risky, but *A* pays out fifty percent of earnings while *B* pays out ten percent of earnings. Then it is alleged that a share of *A*'s stock might sell at a higher price than that of *B*.

This appendix casts doubts on this view by arguing the following surprising and, perhaps, even paradoxical propositions:

1. Even if the relative discount on *B*'s stock remains unchanged at all future dates and the two companies obtain equal and constant earnings on a dollar of investment, a security purchaser will receive a higher return per dollar of his investment if he buys *B* stocks than if he purchases *A* stocks.

2. The differential in accumulated stockholder returns will be greater the longer the period of time during which he holds on to his securities and the larger the ratio of dividend payments to earnings by company *B*.

3. However, in the special case where company *B* pays zero dividends the differential between the returns to the two stocks will disappear.

[1] For the classic statement of this position see the influential Graham and Dodd, *Security Analysis*, 3rd ed. in collaboration with Charles Tatham, Jr. (New York: McGraw-Hill, 1951), pp. 432–6, esp. p. 435. A recent supporting view by an economist may be found in Myron J. Gordon, *The Investment Financing and Valuation of the Corporation* (Homewood, Ill.: R. D. Irwin, 1962), pp. 55–66.

4. If dividends are not zero the market value of the holdings (including his reinvested dividends) of a purchaser of a single share of company *B* will, over time, asymptotically approach the holdings of the purchaser of a share of company *A*, and the rate of approach will be more rapid the greater the dividend payments of company *B*.

5. If dividends are not zero the discounted present value of the stream of prospective dividends (from now into the indefinite future) will be identical for the two securities.

Though a brief intuitive explanation of these results has been offered in the text a more rigorous and explicit discussion seems desirable.

Notation and Assumptions

In proving the preceding results the following notation will be employed:

Let E_t be the earnings per share in period t

$\quad\quad$ D_t be dividends per share in period t

$\quad\quad$ r $\quad$ be the payout ratio, D_t/E_t

$\quad\quad$ k $\quad$ be the rate of earnings on investment (per period)

$\quad\quad$ u $\quad$ be the undervaluation factor for a low dividend security

$\quad\quad$ h $\quad$ be the number of periods for which the security is held.

We will assume in our argument that k, u and r are constant for all periods and all amounts invested or earned. Moreover, we posit

$\quad\quad$ $0<k<1$ (earnings nonzero but less than 100 percent) and

$\quad\quad$ $0<u<1$ (undervalued stocks are not free).

Finally, it will be assumed that the number of shares in each company remains constant.

The Basic Relationships

As a preliminary step in the proof of our theorems, this section derives expressions for the present value of the dividend payments and the value of any one of our stocks if it is held for h periods. In any period $(1-r)E_t$ will be reinvested by the company (the remainder being paid out in dividends). This reinvested sum will earn $k(1-r)E_t$ dollars in the next period, so that earnings in period $t+1$ are given by

$$E_{t+1} = E_t + k(1-r)E_t = (1+k-kr)E_t.$$

This trivial first-order difference equation has the solution
$$E_t = (1+k-kr)^t E_0.$$
Hence, the dividend in period t will be
(1) $$D_t = r(1+k-kr)^t E_0.$$
With a rate of return, k, the discount factor must of course be $1/1+k$, so that the discounted present value of the future stream of dividends received before horizon date h will equal

$$P_h = \sum_{t=0}^{h-1} rE_0[(1+k-rk)/(1+k)]^t = rE_0 \sum_{t=0}^{h-1} \left(1-\frac{rk}{1+k}\right)^t$$

$$= rE_0 \frac{1-\left(1-\frac{rk}{1+k}\right)^h}{\frac{rk}{1+k}}, \text{ that is,}$$

(2) $$P_h = \frac{1+k}{k} E_0 \left[1-\left(1-\frac{rk}{1+k}\right)^h\right].$$

To determine the value of the investor's return at this point in time, however, we must know not only P_h, the present value of his dividends, we must also determine the value of his share at that date. Using the same expression for dividends, (1), and the same discount rate, the expected future dividends to be yielded by our share from period h onward will be (discounting back to the present)

$$\sum_{t=h}^{\infty} rE_0 \left[(1+k-rk)/(1+k)\right]^t$$

$$= rE_0 \left(1-\frac{rk}{1+k}\right)^h \sum_{t=0}^{\infty} \left(1-\frac{rk}{1+k}\right)^t = rE_0 \left(1-\frac{rk}{1+k}\right)^h \frac{1}{\frac{rk}{1+k}}$$

$$= \frac{1+k}{k} E_0 \left(1-\frac{rk}{1+k}\right)^h.$$

This, then, is the present value of the dividends to be obtained by our share from period h onward. If this share is undervalued, then its market value will be reduced by the undervaluation factor u. Adding the resulting expression to (2) the present value of dividend earnings before period h, we have the total value obtained from our share,

$$(3) \qquad V_h = \frac{1+k}{k} E_o \left[1 - \left(1 - \frac{rk}{1+k} \right)^h + u \left(1 - \frac{rk}{1+k} \right)^h \right].$$

In effect, (3) represents the present value of the returns from our share if it is held for h periods and then sold.

Now compare this with the returns from some other share whose pay-out rate, r*, is greater than r, and which is therefore not undervalued. Then, since u = 1, (3) reduces simply to

$$(4) \qquad V_h^* = E_o(1+k)/k$$

which, it will be noted, is independent both of the magnitude of r*, the dividend payout rate, and h, the length of time for which the share is held.

Proof of the Propositions

We may now prove our propositions without difficulty. The initial market value of our undervalued share is, by (3), $V_o = uE_o(1+k)/k$, the present value of its expected earnings, multiplied by the undervaluation factor, u. Hence the present value of the yield per dollar of investment in this share is

$$(5) \qquad V_h/V_o = \frac{1}{u} \left[1 - (1-u) \left(1 - \frac{rk}{1+k} \right)^h \right].$$

Since the present value of the other share's returns is independent of the date at which it is sold, the corresponding return per dollar is, of course, unity. That is, by (4) we have

$$(6) \qquad V_h^*/V_o^* = 1.$$

Proposition 1 now follows immediately. We may rewrite (5) as

$$(7) \qquad V_h/V_o = 1 + \frac{1-u}{u} \left[1 - \left(1 - \frac{rk}{1+k} \right)^h \right] \geq 1.$$

V_h/V_o is greater than unity for $h > 0$ since both u and $\frac{rk}{1+k}$ are then both positive and less than unity. Thus $V_h/V_o > V_h^*/V_o^*$ for $h > 0$ as proposition 1 asserts, so that the "undervalued" share is indeed the better investment even though its rate of undervaluation, u, is fixed over time.

Proposition 2 can be verified by direct inspection of (7) which shows that the return difference $V_h/V_o - V^*_h/V^*_o$ increases with r, the dividend payout rate and with h, the length of time for which the security is held.

Proposition 3 is derived by setting the dividend payout rate, $r = 0$, whence $V_h/V_o = 1$ so that the return of the undervalued stock becomes the same as the return to investment in the other security.

Proposition 4 is obtained from (3) and (4) from which we see

$$V_h^* - V_h = \frac{1+k}{k} E_o(1-u)\left(1 - \frac{rk}{1+k}\right)^h$$

so that the difference between the value obtained from the two shares does approach zero, at a rate which varies directly with the magnitude of r.

Finally, proposition 5 follows by letting h approach infinity in (2) whence we have as the limit value of P_h

$$P = E_o(1+k)/k.$$

Since this is completely independent of the dividend payout rate, r, it shows that all shares with given earnings prospects per dollar of investment will approach the same dividend payments stream in terms of capitalized present value. This last result, which says that if stockholders wait long enough, a low (but non-zero) dividend rate must yield them dividends worth exactly as much as a high dividend rate, is the key to the other results of this appendix—it shows that the dividends paid out of the earnings of reinvested earnings must gradually approach an amount equal in aggregate present value to the dividends which would otherwise have been paid out from current earnings.

Chapter Four

Taskmaster Imperfect

THE STOCK MARKET AS ENGINE OF EFFICIENCY

IN THE PRECEDING CHAPTERS our primary concern has been with the design of the stock market as a mechanism for the efficient allocation of the economy's capital resources. We have asked ourselves whether the superficial resemblance to a competitive structure does as a matter of fact indicate that the stock exchange is characterized by most of the important attributes of a purely competitive market so that it can be relied upon to *allocate* capital in a manner which is approximately optimal. Thus we were concerned to determine who gets the resources. In this chapter we turn to a somewhat related question; how efficiently are these resources employed by their recipients? Or, rather, what role does the stock market play in contributing towards the efficiency of that utilization?

This is no idle question. The role of guardian of efficiency is one which it is natural to expect to be assigned to the stock markets. One would think that the firm which employs funds ineffectively

66

would find itself denied easy access to them by an alert capital market, whereas the efficient user of resources should be able to obtain them cheaply and easily. Thus rewards and punishments would be meted out by the market and management's collective nose kept to the grindstone by anticipated future capital needs.

To some extent the discussion of the preceding chapter bears on these matters also, because the market can only act in the way we have just indicated if the valuation of a company's securities does correspond closely to its future earnings prospects. The most direct measure of its efficiency of operation is the company's stream of earnings; and only by offering high prices for the stocks of the companies whose prospects are brightest can the market provide capital to them on better terms.

But in this chapter we will deal with another aspect of the matter. Even if the machinery which I have just described is available it may be that the economy's institutional arrangements cause it to stand idly by and prevent it from coming to grips with the operations of the inefficient enterprise. The stock market may prove to be an ineffective taskmaster simply because company operations remain beyond its reach. Yet, even if this proves to be so—if the mechanism to which we are alluding comes but rarely into play, we will see that there exist some alternative means whereby the market may be able to serve as a guardian of efficiency of operations.

Utilization of the Market as a Source of Capital for the Firm

Some simple statistics seem to settle rather quickly and conclusively one of the issues which have just been raised: does the market have the opportunity to exercise the *obvious* type of control over the efficiency of operation of the firms whose securities it trades? Apparently it does not. We have already seen in the preceding chapter that new issues—the market's most direct instrument for providing capital to business firms—were negligible in their total amount when compared to the magnitude of securities traded or to the inventories of securities available. In part, this disproportion reflects the huge quantity of stock which has been accumulated out of the past. But it is also a consequence, apparently, of the fact that firms typically and perhaps increasingly have sought to avoid the stock market (along with other external sources) in obtaining their resources. As one writer describes the situation:

... since World War II, only a meager supply of new issues has been offered ... some indication of the relatively insignificant role of equity financing in the postwar period can be obtained from an analysis of the sources and uses of corporate funds since the end of the Second World War. ... Between 1946 and 1959, nonfinancial corporations used on a net basis about $486 billion of funds. Plant and equipment expenditures absorbed $313 billion; $58 billion represented an increase in inventories, and the remaining $115 billion were employed as working capital. Funds from the corporations' own operations, amounting to $298 billion, were sufficient to meet three-fifths of the total required and 95 percent of expenditures on plant and equipment. When these business firms did go outside to obtain funds, they relied on stocks for 7 percent of their total needs, and the amounts raised were only 11 percent of plant and equipment outlays. In contrast, corporate bonds constituted 12 percent of all sources and 18 percent of plant and equipment purchases.[1]

Or, as another author puts it, in a discussion of the data from 1947 through 1961,

One thing that strikes the eye ... is the overwhelming importance of internally-generated capital funds. Over the 15 years [1947–1961] as a whole, they have accounted for *more than 85 percent* of the total. Another thing is their increasing share of the total. They have been generally rising over the interval, while outside funds have fluctuated irregularly with no clear trend. ... One thing is conspicuous: the overwhelming importance of retained earnings as a source of capital growth. They have accounted generally for 60–90 percent of the total, the average for the 15 years being 73 percent. Another conspicuous feature is the relative unimportance of net stock issues. For the period as a whole, they have accounted for *less than 4 percent* of the total growth.[2]

---

[1] Andrew F. Brimmer, *Life Insurance Companies in the Capital Market*, MSU Business Studies (East Lansing: Michigan State University, 1962), pp. 335–8. Reprinted by premission of the publishers.

[2] *Capital Goods Review*, Machinery and Allied Products Institute, No. 50 (July 1962), pp. 2–3. Reprinted by permission of the publishers. The portion of the statement about the rising share of internal sources may be somewhat misleading. As the author points out "their growth has reflected entirely the increase in depreciation allowances [Including amortization. The increase in capital consumption allowances over the interval has been due primarily to the growth of

These striking figures by themselves suffice to indicate that firms have been avoiding the stock market as a major source of capital, and the regulatory powers of the market over the operations of the company are thereby put into question.

But the evidence just cited does not by itself preclude the possibility that *most* companies will find it necessary to turn to the market at times and that even though the proportion of their resources which they obtain from that source is small, it may nevertheless be extremely important to management. That is, if each company obtains 4 percent of its funds from the market and if this 4 percent makes a critical difference, at the margin, to the firm's operations, the stock market may still be able thereby to impose its influence upon the firm. But there is evidence that even this possibility can be ruled out. There is reason to believe that a very substantial proportion of America's large business enterprises manages to avoid recourse to the market altogether, at least for very substantial periods of time. The source of our preceding quotation summarizes a study by Professor Gordon Donaldson in which he investigated the financing of twenty large manufacturing corporations over the twenty-year period, 1939–1958. All of the firms in the sample are public companies, all but three being listed on the New York stock exchange.

Over the entire 20-year period covered by Donaldson's study, 1939–58, seven of the 20 companies generated internally *more than 100 per cent* of their total long-term capital requirements. Five more generated over 95 percent. Another five were in the 80–95 percent range. *Only three fell below 80 percent.*

With respect to the frequency of outside financing, three of the 20 companies did not go to the long-term capital market at all. Of the remainder, 16 borrowed, three of them only once, 5 only twice. Five companies issued preferred stock; 4, common. Only 2 issued common more than once. Only 4 made really intensive use of the capital market. . . .

Of the 363 company-years covered in the study (in three cases data were available for only part of the 20-year period), exactly half (181) showed a surplus of internal funds over requirements. Even more interesting is the

depreciable assets, but has been materially augmented by the accelerated writeoff methods made available by the 1954 code. (Footnote in original)]. Retained earnings have moved sidewise over the period, if indeed they have not trended downward."

fact that in 105 of the 182 deficit years the deficiency was made good without resort to the capital market, by reductions in liquid reserves and by dividend cutbacks.[3]

As Professor Donaldson himself states:

The overwhelming importance of retained earnings and the comparatively infrequent use of stock issues suggests that management was avoiding a common issue as much as possible. . . . Though few companies would go so far as to rule out a sale of common stock under any circumstances, the large majority had not had such a sale in the past 20 years and did not anticipate one in the foreseeable future. *This was particularly remarkable in view of the high price-earnings ratios of recent years.*[4]

He concludes:

Management strongly favors internal generation as a source of new funds even to the exclusion of external sources except for occasional unavoidable "bulges" in the need for funds. Only a small minority push the rate of investment to the point of having a need substantially in excess of internal generation over extended periods of time.[5]

From all of this there appears to be only one inescapable conclusion: that a very substantial proportion of American business firms manage to avoid the *direct* disciplining influences of the securities market, or at least to evade the type of discipline which can be imposed by the provision of funds to inefficient firms only on extremely unfavorable terms. A company which makes no direct use of the stock market as a source of capital can, apparently, proceed to make its decisions confident in its immunity from this type of punishment by the impersonal mechanism of the stock exchange.

On the Theory of Stock Market Avoidance

Though these results are apparently conclusive, it seems appro-

---

[3] *Capital Goods Review*, p. 4.

[4] Gordon Donaldson, *Corporate Debt Capacity* (Boston: Division of Research, Harvard Business School, 1961), pp. 56–8. My italics. Reprinted by permission of the publishers.

[5] *Ibid.*, p. 67. Of course, internal generation of funds may be interpreted as an indirect means to increase equity. Management, then, in effect, increases the holdings of current stockholders by what may be taken to amount to a preemptive issue, rather than going out to look for new customers for its shares.

priate to ponder them a little and to try and arrive at some explanation for this somewhat surprising behavior of the business firm. It is thus appropriate to digress and consider from a theoretical point of view the determination of the optimal quantity of capital to be raised through the agency of the stock market. As has occurred at several points in this book there is an answer which suggests itself at first blush but which, on closer examination, turns out to be a serious oversimplification.

It is frequently held that the cost of funds on the security market falls whenever stock prices rise just as the yield of a bond varies inversely with its price. One would think that it pays management to turn to the market for funds whenever the cost of stock market capital, thus interpreted, falls sufficiently. Specifically, one should apparently invest with the aid of this source whenever that cost of capital falls below the marginal efficiency of investment. As the *Capital Goods Review* comments

As a theoretical proposition, a company should bring in outside capital whenever the investment of the proceeds promises to improve earnings by more than the amount claimed by the added capital. Contrariwise, it should retire existing capital whenever the disinvestment promises to reduce earnings by less than the amount claimed by the capital released. This means that if its internal funds run out at a cutoff rate above the cost of outside capital it should import and invest until the cutoff is brought down to it. It means at the other end that if its internal funds take it down to a cutoff below the yield obtainable from the retirement of existing capital, it should export the excess funds by making such retirements.

As a practical matter, of course, the game cannot be played with the precision that this implies. Capital is not drawn from the market, like water from a tap, at whatever time, and in whatever amount, desired. Neither is it released to the market by a similar procedure in reverse. For reasons known to anyone familiar with the problem, outside financing (other than short-term borrowing) is a major undertaking for most companies, and is engaged in, if at all, at infrequent intervals. Capital retirements are also "lumpy" and irregular. As a result, there can rarely be the nice correspondence between investment opportunities and employed capital called for by theoretical analysis. But certainly most companies can come far closer to the theoretical ideal than they do.[6]

[6] *Op. cit.*, pp. 5–6.

This view of the theory of investment offers no ready explanation for the scant employment by American corporations of funds derived from the stock market during the postwar period when stock prices reached spectacular heights and when price-earnings ratios were at correspondingly extraordinary levels.[7] On this interpretation one can only conclude that the failure to take advantage of the stock market as a very inexpensive source of funds is a manifestation either of business irrationality or of excessive caution or both.

However, if we follow the logic of the Modigliani-Miller analysis, we find once again that we are forced to complicate what appears at first to be a relatively simple problem. Let us consider more carefully the amount of new capital which it will pay firms to acquire from the Exchange.

Given the level of investment, a decision to decrease the amount of retention and internal financing is tantamount to a decision to raise the payment of dividends to shareholders and, concomitantly, to compensate for this by increasing the amount of capital derived from other sources. If, for the sake of simplicity, we deal with a world in which there are only two sources of funds, the stock market and retained earnings, then given the level of investment, every increase in dividend payout necessarily requires a corresponding increase in equity financing. But we have seen in the preceding chapter that in a perfect capital-market world with perfect foresight, a change in the rate of dividend payment offers neither an advantage nor a disadvantage to the current stockholder. That is, since the rate of dividend payout is irrelevant from his point of view, it follows that whatever the earnings-price ratio, the share of the firm's capital which is financed through the agency of the stock market is of no interest to the current shareholder.

But this irrelevance holds only in a perfect world. As imperfections are allowed to creep in, the scales become unbalanced. For some investors, transactions costs make it desirable that there be a steady and substantial flow of dividend payments. If a shareholder lives on his dividends and therefore needs the constant flow of funds for his income payments, the transactions costs involved in disposing on a

[7] However, there does seem to have been a substantial increase in the volume of new offerings during 1961 when terms were presumably very favorable.

regular schedule of a small proportion of his security holdings makes the latter a prohibitively expensive alternative. Thus, even if retained earnings do yield their full value to him in the form of capital gains on his securities he may find that a decision to reduce dividend payments works out to his disadvantage. We conclude that the interests of some stockholders may be served by the use of funds derived from the stock market in preference to increased earnings retention.

But, by and large, it would appear to be advantageous to most stockholders if management acquires its funds by retention where-ever possible. There are several reasons why this should be so. The stockholder who receives dividends which he would rather have had retained can, of course, reinvest them but in doing so he is subjected to two unnecessary burdens. First the investor must pay the broker-age and other transactions costs that are incurred in finding assets in which to invest his dividends, and second, he must pay the taxes to which dividends are subject, taxes which in our country are substan-tially higher than the amounts he would have to pay on equivalent capital gains (on which he may be able to escape tax payment alto-gether if the security is held until death or transferred by tax-exempt gift).[8]

In addition to these indirect burdens imposed on the stockholder by failure to finance through retained earnings there are a number of substantial indirect costs which arise when the outlays of the company in which he holds stocks are increased by the process. To the firm there are three obvious advantages to retained earnings as a source of capital. The heavy transactions costs involved in floating a new issue are thereby avoided, the firm is not forced to seek new purchasers of his securities who, because they have not already bought into the company, are likely to be less anxious to hold these stocks and will therefore only buy them at a discount.[9] Third, because funds can be obtained from the stock market only in discontinuous chunks while

[8] Even where capital gains are taxed, they offer the additional advantage of deferred payment which enables the investor to make use of the funds until the gains are realized.

[9] See John Lintner, "Dividends, Earnings, Leverage, Stock Prices and the Supply of Capital to Corporations," *The Review of Economics and Statistics*, 44 (August 1962), pp. 256–9.

retained earnings flow into the company's coffers continuously and smoothly it is clear that the latter can in this respect constitute a much more economical source of funds for the firm.

Thus from the point of view of the bulk of the body of investors and the preponderance of business firms, the determination of the optimal sources of funds may turn out to be comparatively simple. It would appear that the bulk of business enterprise should finance its investments insofar as possible entirely out of retained earnings *because that is, characteristically, the cheapest way to raise additional funds.* Only when it becomes impossible to provide enough money from internal sources should the firm turn to the stock market or to borrowing for resources. Optimal dividend levels would then be determined residually, providing to stockholders only those funds which the company cannot invest profitably.[10] In effect, the key point is that retention is often the cheapest way for his company to raise what is, in effect, *new equity* capital.

It seems, then, that there are good theoretical grounds which can explain the resistance of business firms to utilization of the stock exchange as a source of funds. Yet I must not pretend that the preceding discussion describes the reasons which are really most significant in practice. One can easily provide a variety of what might be termed "practical" explanations for management's reluctance to turn to the securities market, a number of them well grounded and others rather more questionable. Some of these can be described rather briefly:

1. *Unwillingness to dilute the equity of current stockholders.* This is the argument that the issue of new stocks will reduce the well-being of current stockholders by making a portion of their property rights available to others. The argument is, of course, only valid if the funds acquired in this manner are not invested by the firm in projects which yield a return greater than the cost of its capital (however that may be measured). If the new investments yield a return which exceeds the cost of the new equity funds, the value of the assets held by current stockholders should be increased.

---

[10] There is another reason why it will sometimes be desirable to offer nonzero dividends. As Modigliani and Miller point out ("Reply," *American Economic Review*, 49 September 1959), dividend payments are sometimes management's most effective way of communicating a company's long-run earnings prospects.

2. *The SEC regulations and the transactions costs which they impose.* At least partly because of the time needed to meet the requirements of current regulations, a lag of nearly six months typically intervenes between the time an issue is decided upon and the date when it is brought out. In addition, a huge expenditure may be incurred in providing the information which this agency requires. Though this consideration really falls under the heading of transactions costs, which have already been mentioned, it is sufficiently important to merit somewhat more explicit description.

3. *Other transactions costs.* While discussing transactions cost it is appropriate to list specifically some of its components. These include (a) underwriting cost; (b) registration cost; (c) psychic costs, including liabilities incurred if there is a slip in the process of providing the requisite "full and fair disclosure"; the time spent in preparation of statements and the general upsetting of executives' time tables which may go on for months; (d) disclosure cost—the loss in competitive advantage which is apt to result from the prohibition of financial secrets to the issuing company; (e) the reduction in selling price of company securities which results when a large batch of securities is offered for sale on the market at one time and (f) restrictions on the company's freedom of action which result from any restrictive provisions involved in the issue. It should be fairly clear that these costs alone are likely to make management look with distaste upon the prospect of a trip to the market to acquire additional funds.

4. *Uncertainty.* When a new stock issue is planned it is often difficult to judge in advance just what it will bring in. Here the delays caused by SEC requirements are again relevant. Even though the market may be buoyant at the time an issue is first planned, there is no guarantee that it will continue to be so when it finally appears on the market several months later.

5. *Desire to protect the value of stock options.* Stock options constitute a very significant proportion of the remuneration of corporation executives. They have therefore probably grown into a very powerful motivating force affecting a variety of business decisions. Now, growth in the value of the company's securities clearly serves the interests of the executive who holds such options, and as we have seen (point 1, above) it is sometimes feared that an increase in the supply of the company's stocks will reduce the value of each share and will therefore work to management's disadvantage.

6. *Avoidance of Market Discipline.* The accumulation of funds out of retained earnings occurs quietly and unobtrusively—it does not rock the boat. It does not put management's policies to a public test like that constituted by the sale of a new stock issue on the market. Thus, a new

issue subjects management to risks beyond those incurred by the company, risks which reinforce management's personal disinclination to utilize the market.

Perhaps there are other and equally compelling reasons which have not been included in the list but even by themselves I think it constitutes an impressive set of grounds which, together with the preceding theoretical analysis, indicates that the infrequent use of the Exchange by the American corporation is neither a historical accident nor a manifestation of irrational behavior.

The upshot is that the stock market is only infrequently given the opportunity to discipline directly the vast majority of the nation's leading corporations and that there seems to be little reason to expect imminent and dramatic changes in this circumstance. If we look to the stock market as a direct regulator of the efficiency of America's corporate enterprise we must find other means for it to accomplish this assignment.

Efficiency of Utilization of Investment Funds

Still, there are some companies which do obtain capital from the securities market, some of them even do so fairly frequently or do obtain a significant proportion of their capital from this source. One may reasonably inquire into the consequences for these companies; whether in fact their subjection to the market test forces them to enhance the efficiency of their overall operations. This is an issue which can only be settled by empirical evidence. I can think of no a priori basis on which its discussion can be carried beyond the simple hypothesis that, *ceteris paribus*, companies whose operations are subject to public scrutiny and reward or punishment by the securities exchange should be expected to do better than those who have managed to insulate themselves from such pressures.

A remarkable study conducted by I. M. D. Little[11] offers us some preliminary tidbits which bear on our general subject, the efficiency of utilization of new capital by the business firm. While it tells us nothing about the effects of market discipline, our immediate topic, it does

---

[11] I. M. D. Little, "Higgledy Piggledy Growth," *Bulletin of the Oxford Institute of Statistics*, 24 (November 1962).

suggest how that too might be investigated. Little's statistical methods make no pretense at great sophistication, yet his study has managed to provide tentative conclusions which are as surprising as they are disturbing. Employing data provided by Moody's Services Ltd, Little studied 441 large firms for which a complete record was available for the period from 1951–1959. In addition, he worked with a second sample of 81 smaller enterprises selected at random from Moody's Index of Public Companies. Again he dealt with firms for which there were continuous records from 1951 through 1959 but this time he confined himself to companies whose trading profits did not exceed £250,000 in 1951.

In the portion of Little's study which is most interesting for our purposes, he inquired whether the amount that a firm plows back influences the rate of growth of its earnings. That any one would ask this may be rather surprising in itself. Who would doubt that the firms with the highest plowback rate would also increase their earnings most rapidly? Yet things did not quite turn out that way. From a multiple correlation calculation which undertook to explain growth in earnings in terms of the asset size of the firm and its rate of plowback[12] Little obtained startlingly negative results which he summarized as follows (p. 409):

(a) Of 13 [industrial] groups, the regression coefficient had the wrong sign in eight cases, but the coefficient was significant in none.
(b) Of the 5 groups with the proper sign, only one was significant (Electrical Engineering)—probably a freak result.
(c) For the whole sample of large firms, the sign was both wrong and significant.
(d) For small firms, the sign was wrong but insignificant.

Since the author was obviously somewhat taken aback by these results,[13] he undertook several other tests to check them. These

[12] It should be emphasized that earnings were adjusted to eliminate variations produced by the issue of new shares so that, in essence, he dealt with earnings per share, or earnings accruing to initial stockholders whose money was plowed back into the firm.

[13] As well as by the small percentage of the variance explained—his multiple correlation explained only $\frac{1}{4}$ of one percent of the total variance—on which Little comments, "is this a record?"

produced very similar conclusions and indicated no relationship between plowback and growth. This must be recognized to be a truly remarkable conclusion. It suggests that, from the point of view of stockholders, retained funds are used with astonishing inefficiency. The earnings growth exhibited by firms which do not save is not discernibly different from those of companies whose plowback is heavy. It is hardly necessary to labor the implications of this observation.

The reader will of course have recognized that Little's results have no direct bearing on the fundamental question which was raised at the beginning of this section: whether firms which have recourse to the stock market when they desire additional capital yield better returns to their stockholders than do companies which avoid the market. However, Little's results, besides being interesting in themselves, are important for us in two respects. First of all, they suggest a method of approach which will perhaps enable us to provide at least tentative answers to our question. Second, the outcome of Little's study offers us some grounds for skepticism about *any* simple explanation of earnings differentials. If there is no relationship between growth in earnings per share and plowback, why should we expect that periodic use of the stock market's capital-raising facilities should make a very great deal of difference?

However, one need not rely simply on surmises. Dr. Peggy Heim is currently assembling American data which will enable her to conduct the requisite statistical tests along with tests of some other very interesting hypotheses such as the possibility that, in the allocation of additional funds, firms assign priority to increases in their sales or their total asset holdings rather than to enlarged earnings. Dr. Heim, then, intends to test whether market discipline has in fact served to increase efficiency, that is, whether the earnings returned to funds obtained through the stock market have been significantly higher than those obtained from internal sources. Should the results turn out to be negative, that is, if there is little significant correlation either way (a result which, after Little's experience, will not surprise me greatly) one may well be tempted to question the markets' efficacy as a direct supervisor of the efficiency of utilization of the economy's capital resources.

One might almost venture to conclude on the basis of what has been said so far in this chapter that the market in fact does not allocate much of the economy's capital, and, moreover, what capital it does handle is not utilized with any peculiar efficiency. We seem to have taken the position of the suburbanite who assured his indignant neighbor "I never borrowed your mower and besides it did a miserable job cutting my lawn."

The Market as Indirect Regulator of Efficiency

Unfortunately, as has happened several times before in this book, I am unable to leave a well-defined conclusion alone. Even if the implications of the preceding discussion turn out to be supported completely by the facts, their import is more restricted than it appears on the face of the matter. For, at most, what has been indicated is that the market does not influence *directly* the efficiency of operations of the individual firm. It does not accomplish this end by meting out rewards and punishments in the form of cheaper or more expensive capital funds.

Our arguments, however, do not preclude the existence of more indirect and subtle sanctions which grant fully effective powers of regulation to the exchange. Nor does one have to look very far before being driven to the suspicion that there exist alternatives of this variety. Reports of the deliberations of the top levels of management in major American corporations seem to indicate a widespread concern with the performance of the companies' securities. Even in companies which have long refrained from the issue of new stocks and which apparently have no plans for such an issue in the foreseeable future there seems to be a heavy preoccupation with the market's evaluation of the corporation's shares. Whatever the reasons, and I shall discuss these briefly in a moment, this concern is by itself sufficient to empower the market to oversee the behavior of management. If the businessman is motivated to avoid reductions in the price of his firm's securities and if, in fact, he hopes that those prices will rise rather steadily and dependably with the passage of time, he will be driven to adapt his decisions to this purpose. Behavior which depresses security prices will then conflict with company objectives.

Therefore, if stock price values reflect rather closely the prospective earnings and the efficiency of company operations, the impersonal forces of the market, its invisible hand, will be provided with a very visible club which can keep corporations in line. The evidence on these matters is impressionistic at best. The skeptic may describe it as no more than a collection of anecdotes (which kinder reporters will refer to as "case histories"). Yet one is left with the strong impression that the basic empirical allegation is correct: that it is a rare management which is willing to despise and ignore the market's valuation of its company.

If that is the case, we suddenly find our conclusions to be reversed almost directly. We must take the view that the market does, as a matter of fact, have the power to levy sanctions against the poorly operated firm and that its instruments of control, even if they are not obvious, are not therefore any the less powerful. It is really not so strange that a corporation which obtains little or none of its capital from the stock exchange should nevertheless be concerned with the performance of its securities. It is not difficult to muster a variety of explanations.

As for much of business behavior, perhaps the easiest explanation is public relations. No businessman wishes for advertising that proclaims that his firm has performed unsuccessfully. And, surely, failure is nowhere announced more publicly than it is on the stock market when the price of a company's shares falls severely or for a long period of time.

A still more cogent explanation lies in the residual powers which remain in the hands of the stockholders. Though in much of modern corporate enterprise ownership has effectively been divorced from management so that stockholders have very little control over the day-to-day operations of the firm, it nevertheless remains true that if disaffection among stockholders grows very strong, management's tenure may itself be threatened. A continuing concern of top management is the state of mind of the body of the holders of its securities, and executives will go to considerable trouble to avoid causing displeasure to that group. Clearly, one of the best and most direct ways to make stockholders happy is to make sure that their holdings perform reasonably well, that the prices of the company's stocks rise and rise as quickly as those of other companies.[14]

There is yet a third reason which helps to account for management's preoccupation with company stock prices. The performance of a company's shares can also influence the terms on which it can obtain funds from other sources. For example, lenders are likely to base their risk estimates, and hence their interest terms, in part on the market's evaluation of the corporation's stocks.

But perhaps by far the most important reason for management's concern for the behavior of the price of company stock is the stock option whose value to the recipient executive depends directly on the performance of the company's securities. Though the evidence does not seem to be clear, it has even been alleged that a preponderant share of managerial earnings derives effectively from this source. Thus, self-interest, that most powerful underpinning of the system of free enterprise, must lead management to work for higher prices of the company's stocks.[15] An executive who holds options on 10,000 shares can hardly fail to recognize that a one point rise in the price of the company's stock means $10,000 to him and, in fact constitutes income which is generally taxed at preferential rates. What better device could one possibly have designed to assure management's attention to the current stockholders' capital gains?

Whatever the relative merits of the preceding explanatory hypotheses, there seems little doubt that management, even in those firms which accumulate their capital internally, has good reason to concern

[14] However, the desire to keep stockholders contented may not motivate management to seek to *maximize* the rate of rise of security prices. It may be far better strategy to maintain a steady rate of advance in stock prices, one which can easily be continued in the future rather than producing a spectacular rise in prices which can perhaps not be duplicated later and which may therefore disappoint the expectations to which the initial price increase gave rise. Thus, in management's calculations the requirement that stock prices exhibit a secular growth pattern may take the form of a constraint rather than something which constitutes a prime element in the company's objectives and is therefore to be maximized. But compare the next footnote.

[15] The desire to increase the value of stock options should motivate management to try to *maximize* stock prices and their growth. The stock option may, then, serve as a stronger inducement for increasing the price of securities than does the desire to please the body of stockholders.

itself with the price of the securities of the firm and to avoid any actions which tend to depress those prices. Hence, whether or not the stock market serves as a capital source for the firm and despite the fact that, for the bulk of American enterprise, it only constitutes a capital source of last resort, its powers to police company efficiency may have survived intact.

How effectively it exercises these powers is an empirical question on which I have as yet found little material. The only evidence we have so far seems to be made up of the results of Little's study which were described in an earlier section. It is, perhaps, here that Little's work is most relevant for our analysis. If subsequent investigation confirms that there is very little relationship between plowback and rate of growth of earnings and if a similar conclusion follows from the statistics which pertain to the United States, one will be unable to avoid the suspicion that there is a great deal of waste and inefficiency in the investment process. It can be interpreted to imply that there is something very seriously wrong with the regulatory machinery. Whether this will turn out to be the case still remains to be seen.

Concluding Comments

We have now come to the end of my discussion. We have tried to explore a wide range of subjects, each of which it was hoped would help us to understand the function of the stock market as an allocator of the economy's capital resources. In the process I have sought to integrate the analysis of the workings of the stock market more closely into the framework of standard economic theory and to incorporate into the discussion a number of segments of the theory of corporation finance.

Throughout I have ended up with questions and alternatives rather than with categorical conclusions. We have noted that the workings of the market in some respects resemble those of the competitive model but that in other ways they depart substantially from one another. We have examined arguments which might lead us to expect that security prices would be tied very closely to company earnings prospects and yet other lines of reasoning which imply that the relationship would be haphazard and depend largely on the fortunes of speculation. We have seen that the stock market is not given the opportunity to impose its discipline on the bulk of American corporate enterprise in its role as a capital market, for most firms come but rarely to seek their funds at the Exchange. Yet we have observed that other and perhaps equally powerful instruments of sanction remain to the market.

All in all, one cannot escape the impression that, at best, the allocative function is performed rather imperfectly as measured by the criteria of the welfare economist. The oligopolistic position of those who operate the market, the brokers, the floor traders and the specialists; the random patterns which characterize the behavior of stock prices; the apparent unresponsiveness of supply to price changes and management's efforts to avoid the market as a source of funds, all raise some questions about the perfection of the regulatory operations of the market. But though its workings are undoubtedly imperfect, it does not follow that they are beyond the pale. Rather, its operation must be judged to be somewhat on a par with that of the bulk of America's business. Far from the competitive ideal, beset by a number of patent shortcomings, it nevertheless performs a creditable job. Bearing in mind that its ramifications were never planned by organized human deliberation, one can only marvel at the quality of its performance.

APPENDIX TO CHAPTER FOUR

STOCK OPTIONS AND SEPARATION OF OWNERSHIP FROM MANAGEMENT

Having succumbed to the unattractive habit of frequent digression, it is perhaps fitting that this book be brought to an end by way of one concluding detour on a topic on which the preceding material would seem to cast some light: the effects of the separation of ownership from management.

This subject has aroused widespread interest ever since the appearance of Berle and Means' classic volume.[1] A central implication of

---

[1] Berle, Adolph A., Jr. and Gardiner C. Means, *The Modern Corporation and Private Property* (New York: Macmillan, 1932).

much of the discussion of this subject is that in a large segment of contemporary business enterprise the interests of the capitalists are apt to diverge sharply from those of management. Moreover, it is maintained, this difference can have serious consequences because those who provide the corporation's equity capital have very little to say about the day-to-day operations of the firm. One sometimes almost senses the implication that management can be viewed as a self-serving group whose decisions are prevented from running completely contrary to stockholder interests only by the stock-holders' last recourse—the power of a desperate group of share-holders to remove the current managerial group from office. Of course, no one really holds quite so extreme a view, and the facts of the matter are considerably more mixed than the crudest statements are likely to suggest.

Instead of treating stockholders and managements as two well-defined polar groups each of which is completely homogeneous in its objectives, it is illuminating to recognize that there is usually a variety of stockholder interests which are characterized by differing degrees of approximation to the narrower interests of the officers of the firm.[2] Thus, the body of stockholders constitutes no homogeneous group and if one attempts to determine what promotes the welfare of

[2] One can, for example, distinguish the following categories of stockholder:
1. Officers and directors of the corporation who also hold company stocks;
2. investors who are close to management, if in no other way, by keeping in touch and collecting systematically the considerable amount of information that is available for the asking;
3. investment firms who are influential not only as a result of their careful collection and use of pertinent information, but who provide signals to management by their purchases and sales of company stocks, and who influence other investors both through the agency of investment counsellors, and through the periodic publication of the changes in their own portfolios;
4. the in-and-outers—the active traders who account for a considerable proportion of the market's transactions and who are interested in long-run company prospects only insofar as they are relevant for short-run developments.

One can also distinguish other pertinent stockholder groups with particular interests—those whose advantage is served by a steady stream of dividends, those who prefer capital gains, those who hope to take over control of a company, etc.

"the stockholders" one runs into just the same sort of difficulties as when one undertakes to measure the welfare of society.[3]

It would also seem plausible that the welfare of management is much more closely tied to the well-being of some stockholder groups than it is to others. At the one extreme, what group can be closer to management than the company officers who themselves hold stocks? At the other, the officers of the company will have little affection for a group whose primary goal in becoming stockholders is to effect a takeover. Or—to consider a more common phenomenon—management will feel very little identification with the in-and-outers, and very little responsibility for their welfare.[4]

In practice, then, managements will naturally identify to a different degree with different stockholder groups and separation of ownership from management, instead of amounting to a sharp cleavage, takes the form of a gradual shading-off in the degree of coincidence between managerial and stockholder objectives.

But though there is an affinity between the objectives of at least some stockholders and those of management it does not follow that these interests are identical. Even if both groups wish to move in the same direction they may not move by the same amounts. For example, though maximum profits may best serve stockholder interests, a profit "satisficing" goal—a level of earnings which just suffices to keep stockholders contented—might in the long run be safer for management because there is likely to be less difficulty in maintaining such a more moderate level of accomplishment than in achieving constantly a maximal level of earnings. And, since maximal earnings may well, in

---

[3] This obviously adds to the difficulty of defining the "cost of new capital" if, as usual, one means thereby the opportunity cost to current shareholders as a whole of the acquisition of additional funds by some specified means.

[4] It is not immediately clear that any lack of tender regard for the interests of the in-and-outer can have much operational significance. If the only difference between the in-and-outer and the long-term investor is that the former looks for much shorter term appreciation it would seem that a management which favors the long-term investor group would work harder to improve the company's more distant future. But *if* the value of company stocks is determined by the capitalized present value of *all* future earnings, anything which improves the company's future prospects will cause a corresponding stock price rise at once, unless the information is deliberately withheld.

the nature of the case, exhibit a highly variable time-path it is even conceivable that they might meet with a smaller degree of stock-holder approbation than an intermediate but steady earnings stream. A management whose objective is the quiet life might therefore be tempted to compromise—to avoid trying too hard, lest by its achievements it only stir up trouble for itself.

In practice, the relationship between the self-interests of management and those of stockholders are not left entirely to chance. As is the case with many other occupational groups in our economy, a very substantial segment of management has been put under what amounts to an incentive compensation scheme. For that is the interpretation which we must put on the institutional arrangement whereby a very significant proportion of management's income is provided to it in the form of stock options. Since the value of an option is directly dependent on the value of the company's stocks, whatever enhances the value of the former must also augment that of the latter.

But as we shall see presently, as with most incentive compensation devices, the stock option will at least in some cases produce only an imperfect coincidence between stockholder and managerial interests. In other words, while the option may well remove much of the force of the most extreme separation of ownership and management argument, it does not completely invalidate it. And, as before in this book, I will make no attempt to emerge with final judgment of the relative merits of the two opposing viewpoints. Rather, it is my object to indicate the grounds on which the issue must ultimately be decided, and to draw attention to some aspects of the matter which seem generally to have been overlooked.

Let us begin our discussion by recapitulating the provisions of a stock option. In brief, a stock option entitles its recipient to purchase any number of company shares up to some predetermined maximum (say, no more than 1,000 shares) at a price based on the market value of the shares at the time the option is granted (e.g. 95 percent of their current market price). This option must normally be exercised within some predetermined period, for example, within three years from the initial date. Thus, if the value of the company's stocks rises, the holder of the option can realize a capital gain by purchasing the securities at the fixed option price, and, if he wishes, reselling them at the higher market price which then prevails. Moreover, if he has held the options and the stocks which he purchases through them for a period sufficiently long,[5] these earnings on the transactions can legally qualify as capital gains with all the resulting tax benefits. Indeed, under present law, if the shares are held until death, even the capital gains tax can be escaped altogether. Obviously, then, to the extent that management's remuneration is composed of stock options, it will be motivated to do one thing which serves the interests of most stockholders—it will find it advantageous to work for increases in the value of the company's stocks; specifically, to seek to maximize the magnitude of the increase occurring somewhere within a period long enough to permit the returns to qualify as capital gains though, perhaps, a period not going beyond the time or expiration of the option.

It is, however, important to take note of one form of earning to which the holder of a stock option is *not* entitled. He does not receive any company dividends during the period when he possesses only the option rather than the stocks that it permits him to purchase.

This leads to a theoretical point which, while it may seem a mere technicality, can be highly relevant. Suppose now that there is some optimal level of dividends from the point of view of the stockholder. For example, it might involve their being high enough to supply the steady income stream needed by some of the company's stockholders. Of, if as Modigliani and Miller suggest, dividends serve as the most effective means whereby management can communicate estimates of long-run company earnings prospects then (given past company records) there will at any point in time be an optimal strength of signal (an optimal dividend stream). Or the optimal level of dividends might, in effect, be determined residually by the excess of company earnings over the amount which can profitably be invested in the company. For our present purposes the nature of these optimality

[5] Under the Revenue Act of 1964, if stock options are not to qualify as capital gains they must satisfy the following requirements:
1. when it is acquired, the stock must be held for 3 years;
2. options must not extend beyond 5 years;
3. the price of stock bought by means of the option must be no lower than the market price of the stock at the date the option was issued.

considerations is not crucial. All we require is that there be some positive level of dividends which, in our company, should optimally be paid out to stockholders. Once this is true it follows that the stock option will not normally produce perfect correspondence between managerial and stockholder interests.

To see why this is so, note that if a dollar in dividends contributes an incremental value, K, to the wealth of an option holder, it must certainly contribute more than K dollars to the wealth of someone who holds a share outright. This *must* be so because the former receives no direct dividend payment while the latter does. It follows that any dividend level which is optimal from the point of the option holder will not generally be optimal for the stockholder—a dividend level whose marginal yield to the former is zero must still promise a positive incremental gain to the latter.[6]

The significance of this discussion should not be lost through its relatively abstract formulation. What it has shown, in effect, is that the interests of management and ownership are in many cases reconciled only imperfectly by the stock option device. While the option may guarantee that, on the whole, the goals of both groups call for the same general directions, the option does not rule out differences of very substantial magnitude in the measures required by the two sets of objectives.[7]

Yet there is an important exception, or rather, a case which may

[6] That is, if the functions are differentiable then we must have $\partial W_o/\partial D < \partial W_s/\partial D$ where D is the dividend level, W_o is the wealth claim represented by a stock option and W_s is the wealth accruing to the owner of a share. Hence, if we are dealing with interior rather than corner maxima, a necessary condition for the dividend level which is optimal for the option holder is $\partial W_o/\partial D = 0$. But then we must have $\partial W_s/\partial D > 0$ so that the dividend level will not be maximal for the stockholder.

[7] It may be instructive to note that the difference between the marginal dividend yield to an option holder and that to a stockholder (which has just been discussed) is formally equivalent to the difference between marginal private and social net products encountered in the literature of welfare theory. Thus, if externalities can lead to significant differences between the market equilibrium and the social optimum, it follows that stock options are not guaranteed to prevent comparably large differences between the set of decisions which maximize managerial gains and those which are optimal from the point of view of stockholders.

represent a phenomenon far more normal than it might at first appear. As has already been argued earlier in this chapter, there are important institutional reasons which may make it desirable for many companies to retain as much income as possible, i.e., to keep dividend earnings to a minimum. Specifically, because of the nature of capital gains taxation and because of the considerable transactions costs incurred in raising funds by means other than retention, a company which can profitably invest all of its earnings may well have an optimal dividend level equal to zero—it will serve both stockholder and managerial interests to keep dividend payments down to zero.[8] In that case the preceding argument clearly fails, and at least so far as dividends are concerned, the interests of the stockholders and the option-receiving management will call for identical decisions.

We conclude that any unqualified characterization of the relationship between the goals of a corporation's legal ownership and those of its management is likely to be an oversimplification. The officers of the company, characteristically, are much concerned with the interests of the stockholders, both as a matter of self-interest, and because they take their responsibilities seriously. On the other hand, partly because the interests of the body of stockholders as a whole are not even obviously definable, and because managerial gains are sometimes only imperfectly coordinated with those of stockholders[9] one cannot be sure that what is good for the one group will *always* be good for the other. Rather, one may suspect that at least sometimes, somewhere, managerial groups will be led to rationalize to themselves

[8] In other words, what is suggested here is that in the present context corner maxima need by no means be freakish and unusual.

[9] The argument about dividends and stock options which was just presented is, of course, not the only source of such imperfections. For example, I have argued elsewhere that some risks which are worth while from the stockholders' point of view are likely to be unattractive to management because if they turn out well no special rewards may accrue to the company officers, whereas if they turn out badly, management may be in trouble. Moreover, if it is true [as has been argued statistically by McGuire, Chiu and Elbing ("Executive Incomes, Sales and Profits," *American Economic Review*, 52, September 1962)] that managerial incomes are more closely related to the volume of corporate sales than to profits, the promotion of sales at the expense of profits may be more attractive to management than it is to stockholders.

moves which redound to their own advantage, even though they entail an opportunity loss to stockholders. For the stock option device, while it assures us that the interests of stockholders and management will usually be roughly similar, by no means guarantees that they must always be identical.

Index

Index

American Economic Review, 36n., 60n., 74n., 89n.
American Stock Exchange, 13n., 14n.

Baumol, W. J., 26n., 56n.
Berle, Adolph A., Jr., 83n.
Brimmer, Andrew F., 68n.
Bulletin of the Oxford Institute of Statistics, 76n.

Capital gains, 73, 81, 84, 87, 89
Capital Goods Review (institute publication), 68n., 70n., 71
Capital, national real, 2
Capital resources, allocation of, 1–4, 6–8, 33, 36, 42, 54, 60, 66, 79, 82
Carleton, Willard T., 36n.
"Chicago school," 27
Cootner, Paul H., 39n.
Corporate Debt Capacity (Donaldson), 70n.

dividends, 35n., 54, 55, 55n., 56, 58, 61, 63, 65, 72, 73, 74n., 84, 87, 88, 88n., 89, 89n.
Dodd, David L., 61n.
Donaldson, Gordon, 69, 70n.

Economic Journal, 26n.
Edgeworth, F. Y., 10, 10n.
  box diagram, 23
  theory of tatonnement, see tatonnement
  Walras-Edgeworth mechanism, 11
Elements of Pure Economics (Walras), 10n.
equilibrium value, 9, 22, 23, 28, 48, 48n., 49
  Edgeworth box diagram, 23
Essays in Positive Economics (Friedman), 26n.

Fama, Eugene F., 41n.
Fisher, L., 41n.
Friedman, Milton, 26n.
Friend, Irwin, 60